D0516639

501
READING
COMPREHENSION
QUESTIONS

501
READING
COMPREHENSION
QUESTIONS

3rd Edition

LEARNINGEXPRESS®

NEW YORK

31143007811046
428.43 Five
501 reading comprehension
questions.
3rd ed.

Copyright © 2006 Learning Express, LLC.

All rights reserved under International and Pan-American Copyright Conventions.
Published in the United States by LearningExpress, LLC, New York.

Library of Congress Cataloging-in-Publication Data:
501 reading comprehension questions—3rd ed.
    p. cm.
  ISBN 978-1-57685-540-9
  1. Reading comprehension—Problems, exercises, etc. I. LearningExpress (Organization).
II. Title: Five hundred one reading comprehension questions.
III. Title: Five hundred and one reading comprehension questions.
LB1050.45.A15 2006
372.47—dc22

                                                                        2005035216

ISBN 978-1-57685-540-9

Printed in the United States of America

9 8 7 6 5 4

Third Edition

For information or to place an order, contact LearningExpress at:
    55 Broadway
    8th Floor
    New York, NY 10006

Or visit us at:
    www.learnatest.com

Contents

Introduction

re you having trouble with reading comprehension questions on tests? Do you want to know how to improve your reading ability or pass placement tests in school or work? If so, then this book is for you. Read on to find out why.

Maybe you already like to read and want to use this book to sharpen your skills for an important test. If so, that's fine. In fact, you can skip this part of the Introduction—or skip the Introduction entirely—and go straight to the questions.

But maybe you're one of the millions of people who have trouble with reading, especially with reading carefully while reading quickly. If so, this Introduction will give you some direction.

First, know that you're not alone. It's a fact that some people relate more easily to numbers or to working with their hands. Still, no other general skill is used more regularly—in work, play, and just plain living—than reading. The good news is that reading well is a skill that can be developed with practice. This book will help, but something else will help even more: If you're serious about developing your reading comprehension skills, go to the library or a bookstore and pick out books on subjects you find fascinating.

For instance, if your interests are in skydiving, biking, golf, scuba diving, race cars, camping, woodworking, or even the stock market, use that as a starting point, and choose a book. The subject will undoubtedly draw you in because you are already interested. Begin to read. You will find that as you focus on the subject matter, you will already know some of the information. But chances are you will discover something new as you read, and you can connect this with your prior knowledge. Eventually, your store of information becomes quite admirable. Repeat the process over and over again. As you do, you will improve your reading comprehension skills, and it won't even seem like a chore.

▶ A Look at Our Book

The first five sections cover the basics—from vocabulary to topic sentences. *501 Reading Comprehension Questions, 3rd Edition* begins with vocabulary because that's what you need to read—the essential building blocks. You will find vocabulary questions, that test your ability to find definitions and context clues. Next, the analogy questions take you a step further. When answering analogy questions, you will learn to develop your ability to compare and contrast, find similarities and differences, and relate parts to whole pieces. Just in case you're wondering why this is important, you should know that the skills you develop from these short exercises in word play will assist you when you are reading longer passages.

As the book progresses, you will be asked to read short, interesting paragraphs to find main ideas and topic sentences. Once you are comfortable with these basic skills, proceed to the passages in the last five sections. This is where you will use your skills to tackle longer passages.

The last five sections begin with one- to two-paragraph passages. Questions following these passages ask you to identify details and facts, choose the main idea, make inferences, or analyze and interpret the text. The passages, both fiction and nonfiction, get longer as you progress through the book, and they all have varied subjects.

Some are about computers, geology, or geography, while others are about poems, philosophy, literature, or art. You will even find some charts and graphs. To make sure you pay close attention, you may want to take notes as you read. This technique of interacting with the text is good to use anytime you read or when you take a test that includes reading comprehension.

The answers to every question are at the back of the book. Each answer is fully explained, so if you have trouble with a particular question, you will be able to figure out how to arrive at the correct answer.

▶ How to Use Our Book

This book is best used to build your critical reading and thinking skills, but you might want to support it with some other LearningExpress Skill Builders Practice books. When it comes to perfecting your reading comprehension, don't ignore any of the other language skills. You will find *Writing Skills Success in 20 Minutes a Day, Vocabulary and Spelling Success in 20 Minutes a Day, 501 Logic and Reasoning Problems,* and *1001 Vocabulary and Spelling Questions* to be indispensable guides. In any case, the more you use the language and understand the building blocks, the easier and faster you will breeze through those reading comprehension passages that you find on most tests.

Working on Your Own

If you are working alone to brush up on the basics and prepare for a test in connection with a job or school, you will want to develop a time schedule and know your learning style. Since everyone reads differently, the number of words or pages you can cover in a given time period may be more or less than one section of this book. That's OK. Just spend 20 minutes—more or less—reading the material and going through the exercises. Don't worry about how much material you're covering. It's important that you're practicing, and chances are that your speed will improve as you go through the book. Your job is to find your pace.

Then, know your learning style. Do you learn best in a quiet room, or do you need music in the background? Whatever the case may be, find the location that best suits you. Do you need to take notes to remember facts and details? Have a pen, pencil, highlighter, and notebook ready. Are you at your best early in the morning or late at night? Pick the best time, get comfortable, and begin.

Tutoring Others

501 Reading Comprehension Questions, 3rd Edition will work well in combination with almost any basic reading or English text. You will probably find it most helpful to give your student(s) a brief lesson on the topic (main idea, fact/detail, inference, etc.), and then have them spend the remainder of the class or session reading the passages and answering the questions. When you finish, take some time for a brief review session.

Stress the importance of learning by doing. Carry a book into class and talk about what you've read so far. Let them know that reading is enjoyable, and they may just use you as a role model!

▶ Suggested Reading List

This section wouldn't be complete without a list of some great books to read. Reading about reading and answering test questions is fine, but the best way to improve your reading ability is to read. This list is compiled by category. Help yourself. Choose one from the list, pick it up at a local bookstore or library, open the cover, and enjoy.

Autobiography/Memoir

Angela's Ashes by Frank McCourt
Autobiography of Malcolm X by Malcolm X
Black Boy by Richard Wright
The Diary of Anne Frank by Anne Frank
Having Our Say by Sarah L. and Elizabeth Delany
The Heroic Slave by Frederick Douglass
I Know Why the Caged Birds Sing by Maya Angelou
Reading Lolita in Tehran: A Memoir in Books
    by Azar Nafisi

Coming of Age

The Catcher in the Rye by J.D. Salinger
The House on Mango Street by Sandra Cisneros
A Separate Peace by John Knowles

Detective/Thriller

Agatha Christie's murder mysteries
The "*A is for…*" series by Sue Grafton
The Client by John Grisham
Sherlock Holmes by Sir Arthur Conan Doyle
The Shining by Stephen King
Watcher by Dean R. Koontz

Fantasy

The Hobbit by J.R.R. Tolkien
On a Pale Horse by Piers Anthony
Any *Harry Potter* book by J.K. Rowling

Historical/Social Issues

The Clan of the Cave Bear by Jean M. Auel
The Color Purple by Alice Walker
The Curious Incident of the Dog in the Night-Time
    by Mark Haddon
Everything is Illuminated by Jonathan Safran Foer
To Kill a Mockingbird by Harper Lee
The Lord of the Flies by William Golding
Of Mice and Men and *The Grapes of Wrath*
    by John Steinbeck
Schindler's List by Thomas Keneally
The Secret Life of Bees by Sue Monk Kidd
White Teeth by Zadie Smith

Inspirational/Spiritual

Care of the Soul by Thomas Moore
The Five People You Meet in Heaven
    by Mitch Albom
*The Purpose-Driven Life: What on Earth Am
    I Here For* by Rick Warren
A Simple Path by Mother Theresa
The Tao of Pooh and *The Te of Piglet*
    by Benjamin Hoff
The Tibetan Book of Living and Dying
    by Sogyal Rinpoche

Mythology

Mythology by Edith Hamilton

The Power of Myth by Joseph Campbell

American Indian Myths and Legends
by Richard Erdoes and Alfonso Ortiz

Poetry

*The Norton Anthology of Modern Poetry: Second
Edition* edited by Richard Ellmann and
Robert O'Clair

Science Fiction

1984 by George Orwell

Fahrenheit 451 or *The Martian Chronicles*
by Ray Bradbury

Jurassic Park by Michael Crichton

The Left Hand of Darkness by Ursula Le Guin

This Perfect Day by Ira Levin

Stranger in a Strange Land by Robert Heinlein

Science/Medicine

Blink: The Power of Thinking Without Thinking
by Malcolm Gladwell

*Freakonomics: A Rogue Economist Explores the
Hidden Side of Everything* by Steven D. Levitt
and Stephen J. Dubner

The Lives of a Cell by Lewis Thomas

*Longitude: The True Story of a Lone Genius Who
Solved the Greatest Scientific Problem of all Time*
by Dava Sobel

Mortal Lessons by Richard Selzer

Short Stories

Any short story by Ernest Hemingway or O. Henry

Girls at War by Chinua Achebe

Interpreter of Maladies by Jhumpa Lahiri

The Stories of Eva Luna by Isabel Allende

Ten Top Stories edited by David A. Sohn

War

All Quiet on the Western Front by Erich
Maria Remarque

Hiroshima by John Hersey

The Red Badge of Courage by Stephen Crane

SECTION

1 ▶ Vocabulary

Understanding the words used to construct sentences is the best way to begin practicing for a reading comprehension test. Using a dictionary is, of course, the best way to define a word. But if you're in a testing situation and you are not allowed to use one, rely on the context clues in the sentence. The term *context clues* means that other words in the sentence "give away" or give clues to the definition. For example, sometimes you will find synonyms (words that mean the same thing) or antonyms (words that mean the opposite), or details that lead you to identify the vocabulary word in question. Once in a while, you will find a group of words set off by commas (called an appositive), which gives you a very clear definition of the word.

The answers to this section begin on page 131.

Read the following sentences and try to choose the best definition for the italicized word by searching for context clues in the sentence.

1. The designer window treatments in her house, installed 17 years ago, were *outmoded*.
   a. unnecessary
   b. pointless
   c. out-of-date
   d. worthless

2. Although the professor's lectures were regarded by many as so *wearisome* that they regularly put students to sleep, he ignored all criticism and refused to make any changes.
   a. modest
   b. unpleasant
   c. boring
   d. objectionable

3. The baseball player's malice toward the referee was revealed in his *spiteful* remarks to the media, which almost ruined the referee's career.
   a. vindictive
   b. crazy
   c. rude
   d. unpleasant

4. Although Zachary is much too inexperienced for the managerial position, he is a willful young man and *obdurately* refuses to withdraw his application.
   a. foolishly
   b. reluctantly
   c. constantly
   d. stubbornly

5. His neighbor's *superficial* remarks trivialized the property line dispute and infuriated Malcolm.
   a. enraged
   b. petty
   c. insulting
   d. misleading

6. When Katya refused to lie to her parents about where she was spending the night, she was completely *ostracized* by her usually loyal friends, who had never shunned her before.
   a. excluded
   b. hurt
   c. cheered
   d. helped

7. Her fashion sense was usually described as *flamboyant*, but on the night of the party, Tanya's outfit was uncharacteristically modest.
   a. impeccable
   b. showy
   c. sloppy
   d. unassuming

8. Mr. Powers was so *gullible* that he believed even the most outlandish excuses of his insincere employees.
   a. intelligent
   b. naïve
   c. dishonest
   d. critical

9. You cannot become a certified teacher without completing the *prerequisite* student teaching assignment.
   a. required
   b. optional
   c. preferred
   d. advisable

10. Charles, aware of his susceptibility to gum disease, is *diligent* about flossing.
a. uncomfortable
b. excited
c. thorough
d. ambivalent

11. Even though she'd read her supervisor's memo four or five times, she still found his rambling message *ambiguous*.
a. profound
b. inspiring
c. ridiculous
d. unclear

12. Excited about winning the award, Marcia walked up to the podium and delivered an *animated* acceptance speech.
a. abbreviated
b. courteous
c. reserved
d. lively

13. The *intermittent* rain soaked the garden many different times during the day.
a. protracted
b. periodic
c. incredulous
d. light

14. In order to get their votes in the next election, the senator responded to all the complaints of her constituents in a *diplomatic* manner.
a. tactful
b. dismissive
c. delaying
d. elaborate

15. After several small brushfires at the campground, officials felt the need to *augment* the rules pertaining to campfires.
a. criticize
b. retract
c. consider
d. expand

16. As soon as the details of the election were released to the media, the newspaper was *inundated* with calls—far too many to be handled effectively.
a. provided
b. bothered
c. rewarded
d. flooded

17. The Marion Police Department's policy of aggressively recruiting women officers is unmatched, *unique* in every way.
a. rigorous
b. admirable
c. unparalleled
d. remarkable

18. When people heard that timid Bob had taken up skydiving, they were *incredulous*.
a. fearful
b. outraged
c. convinced
d. disbelieving

19. The technical department enthusiastically hired Ms. Long because she was *proficient* in the use of computers.
a. sincere
b. adequate
c. competent
d. skilled

20. Even under tremendous public pressure, the planning committee would not commit itself wholeheartedly to the proposal and gave only *tentative* approval to the waterfront development plan.
a. provisional
b. ambiguous
c. unnecessary
d. total

21. Regarding the need for more free refreshments, the group's opinion was enthusiastic and *unanimous*.
a. divided
b. uniform
c. adamant
d. spirited

22. Since the townspeople were so dissatisfied, various methods to *alleviate* the situation were debated.
a. ease
b. tolerate
c. clarify
d. intensify

23. The assistant was fast becoming an *indispensable* member of the department, so they had no choice but to offer him a higher salary to stay on.
a. determined
b. experienced
c. essential
d. creative

24. The attorney wanted to *expedite* the process, because her client was becoming impatient.
a. accelerate
b. evaluate
c. reverse
d. justify

25. The suspect gave a *plausible* explanation for his presence at the scene, so the police decided to look elsewhere for the perpetrator of the crime.
a. unbelievable
b. credible
c. insufficient
d. apologetic

26. He based his conclusion on what he *inferred* from the evidence, not on what he actually observed.
a. predicted
b. imagined
c. surmised
d. implied

27. The neighborhood-watch group presented its *ultimatum* at the town board meeting: Repave the streets or prepare for protests.
a. earnest plea
b. formal petition
c. solemn promise
d. non-negotiable demand

28. The editor of the newspaper needed to be sure the article presented the right information, so his review was *meticulous*.
a. delicate
b. painstaking
c. superficial
d. objective

29. The general public didn't care about the trial and was *apathetic* about the verdict.
a. enraged
b. indifferent
c. suspicious
d. saddened

30. The doctors were pleased that their theory had been *fortified* by the new research.
a. reinforced
b. altered
c. disputed
d. developed

31. The captain often *delegated* responsibility to his subordinates, so as to have time to do the important tasks himself.
a. analyzed
b. respected
c. criticized
d. assigned

32. The news about toxic waste dumping *aroused* the anger of the many listeners of a news broadcast.
a. informed
b. appeased
c. provoked
d. deceived

33. The spokesperson must *articulate* the philosophy of an entire company so that outsiders can understand it completely.
a. trust
b. refine
c. verify
d. express

34. The new shipping and receiving building is an *expansive* facility, large enough to meet our growing needs.
a. obsolete
b. meager
c. spacious
d. costly

35. The attorneys were now certain they could not win the case, because the ruling had proved to be so *detrimental* to their argument.
a. decisive
b. harmful
c. worthless
d. advantageous

36. My brother drives us crazy by *crooning* in the shower.
a. hooting
b. bellowing
c. crying
d. shouting

37. The emotional *fallout* from a natural disaster can adversely affect the residents in a community for years.
a. conflict
b. issues
c. relationship
d. consequences

38. The air in the rainforest was *humid*, making the heat seem even more smothering than before.
a. hot
b. damp
c. hazy
d. volatile

39. The balloon, loose from its string, rose up into the sky, a shiny purple *sphere*.
a. circle
b. globe
c. ovoid
d. nodule

40. After the storm caused raw sewage to seep into the ground water, the Water Department had to take measures to *decontaminate* the city's water supply.
   a. refine
   b. revive
   c. freshen
   d. purify

41. The mayor *tailored* his speech to suit the crowd of homeless people gathered outside his office.
   a. intoned
   b. expanded
   c. altered
   d. shortened

42. The volcano lays *dormant* now, but we feel sure it will erupt again within the year.
   a. inactive
   b. slack
   c. elevated
   d. inattentive

43. Because of his disregard for the king's laws, the prince was punished by being *banished* from the kingdom.
   a. apart
   b. kidnapped
   c. exiled
   d. spirited

44. I *relinquished* my place in line to go back and talk with my friend Diane.
   a. defended
   b. yielded
   c. delayed
   d. remanded

45. I wrote in my *journal* every day, hoping in the future to author a book about my trip to Paris.
   a. notebook
   b. chapbook
   c. diary
   d. ledger

46. The thief *jostled* me in a crowd and was thus able to pick my pocket.
   a. mugged
   b. bumped
   c. assailed
   d. hindered

47. While we traveled in Italy, we stayed in an inexpensive *hostel*.
   a. inn
   b. compound
   c. home
   d. four-star hotel

48. My friend asked me to lie for her, but that is against my *philosophy*.
   a. principles
   b. regulations
   c. personality
   d. introspection

Choose the best vocabulary word for questions 49–51.

49. We had no idea who the special guest speaker would be, because the organizers of the event were so _____.
   a. animated
   b. secretive
   c. talented
   d. emotional

50. When Carson suddenly quit his job, he didn't even _____ how difficult it might be to find a new one.
   a. endorse
   b. require
   c. consider
   d. alter

51. Maggie was the most talented tennis player at her school, even though she'd never had the _____ to take formal lessons.
   a. opportunity
   b. compassion
   c. arrogance
   d. marketability

Questions 52 and 53 are based on the following paragraph.

Rhesus monkeys use facial expressions to communicate with each other and to enforce social order. For example, the "fear grimace," although it looks ferocious, is actually given by a _____ monkey who is intimidated by a _____ member of the group.

52. What is the meaning of the underlined word *grimace* as it is used in the passage?
   a. wrinkle
   b. contortion
   c. shriek
   d. simper

53. Which pair of words, if inserted into the blanks in sequence, makes the most sense in the context of the passage?
   a. calm . . . aggressive
   b. dominant . . . subordinate
   c. confident . . . fearless
   d. subordinate . . . dominant

Questions 54 and 55 are based on the following paragraph.

In prolonged space flight, besides the obvious hazards of meteors, rocky <u>debris</u>, and radiation, astronauts will have to deal with muscle <u>atrophy</u> brought on by weightlessness; therefore, when they return to Earth, they face a protracted period of weight-training to rebuild their strength.

54. What is the most likely meaning of the underlined word *debris* as it is used in this passage?
   a. fragments
   b. decay
   c. bacteria
   d. alien life

55. The underlined word *atrophy*, as used in the paragraph, most nearly means
   a. pain.
   b. wasting.
   c. weakening.
   d. cramping.

Question 56 is based on the following paragraph.

Most of the women in the orchestra wore conventional black skirts and white shirts during concerts and had their hair neatly pulled back. Robin, with her brightly colored clothing and unusual hairstyles, was considered quite <u>eccentric</u>.

56. What is the meaning of the underlined word *eccentric* as it is used in the sentence?
   a. unconventional
   b. joyful
   c. unreliable
   d. proud

Questions 57, 58, and 59 are based on the following paragraph.

The Sami are an indigenous people living in the northern parts of Norway, Sweden, Finland, and Russia's Kola peninsula. Originally, the Sami religion was <u>animistic</u>; that is, for them, nature and natural objects had a conscious life, a spirit. Therefore, one was expected to move quietly in the wilderness and avoid making a disturbance out of <u>courtesy</u> to these spirits. Ghengis Khan is said to have declared that the Sami were one people he would never try to fight again. Because the Sami were not warriors and did not believe in war, they simply disappeared in times of conflict. They were known as "peaceful retreaters."

57. Based on the tone of the passage, which of the following words best describes the author's attitude toward the Sami people?
   a. admiring
   b. pitying
   c. contemptuous
   d. patronizing

58. The closest meaning of the underlined word *animistic*, as it is used in the passage, is
   a. the irrational belief in supernatural beings.
   b. the belief that animals and plants have souls.
   c. the belief that animals are gods.
   d. the primitive belief that people can be reincarnated as animals.

59. What is the meaning of the underlined word *courtesy* as it is used in the passage?
   a. timidity
   b. caution
   c. respect
   d. fear

Analogies

The dictionary defines an *analogy* as a "similarity in some respects between things that are otherwise dissimilar." In each of the questions contained in this section, you will find a pair of related words. Look at those words and try to figure out how they are connected to one another. For example, what is the connection between the words *fish* and *scales*? Obviously, a fish is covered with scales; now think of two other words that share a similar relationship. A good example of this would be *bird* and *feathers*. The similarity between these two unrelated pairs of words is an analogy. The best way to approach an analogy question is to make up a sentence that describes the relationship between the first two words and find another pair in the choices that would fit into that same sentence. A fish *is covered with* scales, as a bird *is covered with* feathers.

The answers to this section begin on page 133.

See how many of the following questions you can answer correctly.

60. PETAL : FLOWER
   a. recliner : chair
   b. leaf : tree
   c. basket : ball
   d. material : fabric
   e. avocado : guacamole

61. SHELF : BOOKCASE
   a. arm : leg
   b. stage : curtain
   c. bench : chair
   d. key : piano
   e. lamp : bulb

62. FISH : SCHOOL
   a. wolf : pack
   b. tiger : jungle
   c. herd : peacock
   d. raven : school
   e. dog : collie

63. SCALE : WEIGHT
   a. yardstick : length
   b. width : depth
   c. length : width
   d. size : area
   e. mileage : speed

64. WATERMELON : FRUIT
   a. collar : leash
   b. dog : companion
   c. fish : bowl
   d. Dalmatian : canine
   e. apple : orange

65. FOOT : SKATEBOARD
   a. tire : automobile
   b. lace : shoe
   c. ounce : scale
   d. walk : jump
   e. pedal : bicycle

66. STRETCH : EXTEND
   a. tremble : roll
   b. thirsty : drink
   c. shake : tremble
   d. stroll : run
   e. stitch : tear

67. KANGAROO : MARSUPIAL
   a. salmon : mollusk
   b. zebra : horse
   c. rhinoceros : pachyderm
   d. beagle : feline
   e. grasshopper : rodent

68. STARVING : HUNGRY
   a. neat : thoughtful
   b. towering : cringing
   c. progressive : regressive
   d. happy : crying
   e. depressed : sad

69. DERMATOLOGIST : ACNE
   a. psychologist : neurosis
   b. child : pediatrician
   c. ophthalmologist : fracture
   d. oncologist : measles
   e. allergies : orthopedist

70. FRAME : PICTURE
   a. display : museum
   b. shelf : refrigerator
   c. mechanic : electrician
   d. nail : hammer
   e. fence : backyard

71. SEARCH : FIND
   a. sleep : wake
   b. explore : discover
   c. draw : paint
   d. think : relate
   e. walk : run

72. PHARMACY : DRUGS
   a. mall : store
   b. doctor : medicine
   c. bakery : bread
   d. supermarket : discount store
   e. toys : games

73. LAYER : TIER
   a. section : segment
   b. dais : speaker
   c. curtain : stage
   d. chapter : verse
   e. cotton : bale

74. METROPOLITAN : URBAN
   a. bucolic : rural
   b. sleepy : nocturnal
   c. agricultural : cow
   d. autumn : harvest
   e. agrarian : generous

75. TEACHER : SCHOOL
   a. actor : role
   b. mechanic : engine
   c. jockey : horse
   d. judge : courthouse
   e. author : book

76. PERSIAN : CAT
   a. alligator : crocodile
   b. zebra : reptile
   c. parakeet : bird
   d. rat : marsupial
   e. fly : bee

77. RUN : JOG
   a. trot : race
   b. swim : dive
   c. dance : ballet
   d. juggle : bounce
   e. rain : drizzle

78. SKEIN : YARN
   a. squeeze : lemon
   b. fire : coal
   c. ream : paper
   d. tree : lumber
   e. plow : acre

79. TAILOR : SUIT
   a. scheme : agent
   b. edit : manuscript
   c. revise : writer
   d. mention : opinion
   e. implode : building

80. CONDUCTOR : ORCHESTRA
   a. jockey : mount
   b. thrasher : hay
   c. driver : tractor
   d. skipper : crew
   e. painter : house

81. JAUNDICE : LIVER
   a. rash : skin
   b. dialysis : kidney
   c. smog : lung
   d. valentine : heart
   e. imagination : brain

82. COBBLER : SHOE
   a. jockey : horse
   b. contractor : building
   c. mason : stone
   d. cowboy : boot
   e. potter : paint

83. PHOBIC : FEARFUL
  a. finicky : thoughtful
  b. cautious : emotional
  c. envious : desiring
  d. shy : familiar
  e. ridiculous : silly

84. INTEREST : OBSESSION
  a. mood : feeling
  b. weeping : sadness
  c. dream : fantasy
  d. plan : negation
  e. highlight : indication

85. MONK : DEVOTION
  a. maniac : pacifism
  b. explorer : contentment
  c. visionary : complacency
  d. rover : wanderlust
  e. philistine : culture

86. SLAPSTICK : LAUGHTER
  a. fallacy : dismay
  b. genre : mystery
  c. satire : anger
  d. mimicry : tears
  e. horror : fear

87. VERVE : ENTHUSIASM
  a. loyalty : duplicity
  b. devotion : reverence
  c. intensity : color
  d. eminence : anonymity
  e. generosity : elation

88. SOUND : CACOPHONY
  a. taste : style
  b. touch : massage
  c. smell : stench
  d. sight : panorama
  e. speech : oration

89. CONVICTION : INCARCERATION
  a. reduction : diminution
  b. induction : amelioration
  c. radicalization : estimation
  d. marginalization : intimidation
  e. proliferation : alliteration

90. DELTOID : MUSCLE
  a. radius : bone
  b. brain : nerve
  c. tissue : organ
  d. blood : vein
  e. scalpel : incision

91. UMBRAGE : OFFENSE
  a. confusion : penance
  b. infinity : meaning
  c. decorum : decoration
  d. elation : jubilance
  e. outrage : consideration

92. PROFESSOR : ERUDITE
  a. aviator : licensed
  b. inventor : imaginative
  c. procrastinator : conscientious
  d. overseer : wealthy
  e. moderator : vicious

93. DEPENDABLE : CAPRICIOUS
  a. fallible : cantankerous
  b. erasable : obtuse
  c. malleable : limpid
  d. capable : inept
  e. incorrigible : guilty

94. FROND : PALM
  a. quill : porcupine
  b. blade : evergreen
  c. scale : wallaby
  d. tusk : alligator
  e. blade : fern

95. METAPHOR : SYMBOL
   a. pentameter : poem
   b. rhythm : melody
   c. nuance : song
   d. slang : usage
   e. analogy : comparison

96. DIRGE : FUNERAL
   a. chain : letter
   b. bell : church
   c. telephone : call
   d. jingle : commercial
   e. hymn : concerto

97. FERAL : TAME
   a. rancid : rational
   b. repetitive : recurrent
   c. nettlesome : annoying
   d. repentant : honorable
   e. ephemeral : immortal

98. SPY : CLANDESTINE
   a. accountant : meticulous
   b. furrier : rambunctious
   c. lawyer : ironic
   d. shepherd : garrulous
   e. astronaut : opulent

99. DOMINANCE : HEGEMONY
   a. romance : sympathy
   b. furtherance : melancholy
   c. independence : autonomy
   d. tolerance : philanthropy
   e. recompense : hilarity

100. AERIE : EAGLE
   a. capital : government
   b. bridge : architect
   c. unit : apartment
   d. kennel : veterinarian
   e. house : person

▶ Main Ideas, Themes

Finding the *main idea* or *theme* of a written piece is one of the most important aspects of good reading comprehension. It is, however, easy to confuse the *main idea* or *theme* with the *subject*. Basically, the *subject* of a piece of writing is what that piece is *generally* about, plain and simple— the facts and information. However, when you look past the facts and information to the heart of what writers are trying to say, and why they are saying it, that's the *main idea* or *theme*. For example, the *subject* of this introduction is about distinguishing between a *subject* and a *main idea* or *theme*; the *main idea* or *theme* is *why* it's important to be able to recognize that difference.

The answers to this section begin on page 134.

Read the following paragraphs and carefully determine what the *main idea* is for each. The best way to approach these questions is to first read the paragraph and then, in your own words, restate what you think the author is trying to say. From the five choices, select the one statement that best supports the author's point.

> If you're a fitness walker, there is no need for a commute to a health club. Your neighborhood can be your health club. You don't need a lot of fancy equipment to get a good workout either. All you need is a well-designed pair of athletic shoes.

101. This paragraph best supports the statement that
   a. fitness walking is a better form of exercise than weight lifting.
   b. a membership in a health club is a poor investment.
   c. walking outdoors provides a better workout than walking indoors.
   d. fitness walking is a convenient and valuable form of exercise.
   e. poorly designed athletic shoes can cause major foot injuries.

> One New York publisher has estimated that 50,000 to 60,000 people in the United States want an anthology that includes the complete works of William Shakespeare. And what accounts for this renewed interest in Shakespeare? As scholars point out, the psychological insights he portrays in both male and female characters are amazing even today.

102. This paragraph best supports the statement that
   a. Shakespeare's characters are more interesting than fictional characters today.
   b. people today are interested in Shakespeare's work because of the characters.
   c. academic scholars are putting together an anthology of Shakespeare's work.
   d. New Yorkers have a renewed interested in the work of Shakespeare.
   e. Shakespeare was a psychiatrist as well as a playwright.

> Critical reading is a demanding process. To read critically, you must slow down your reading and, with pencil in hand, perform specific operations on the text. Mark up the text with your reactions, conclusions, and questions. When you read, become an active participant.

103. This paragraph best supports the statement that
   a. critical reading is a slow, dull, but essential process.
   b. the best critical reading happens at critical times in a person's life.
   c. readers should get in the habit of questioning the truth of what they read.
   d. critical reading requires thoughtful and careful attention.
   e. critical reading should take place at the same time each day.

There are no effective boundaries when it comes to pollutants. Studies have shown that toxic insecticides that have been banned in many countries are riding the wind from countries where they remain legal. Compounds such as DDT and toxaphene have been found in remote places like the Yukon and other Arctic regions.

104. This paragraph best supports the statement that
   a. toxic insecticides such as DDT have not been banned throughout the world.
   b. more pollutants find their way into polar climates than they do into warmer areas.
   c. studies have proven that many countries have ignored their own anti-pollution laws.
   d. DDT and toxaphene are the two most toxic insecticides in the world.
   e. even a worldwide ban on toxic insecticides would not stop the spread of DDT pollution.

The Fourth Amendment to the Constitution protects citizens against unreasonable searches and seizures. No search of a person's home or personal effects may be conducted without a written search warrant issued on probable cause. This means that a neutral judge must approve the factual basis justifying a search before it can be conducted.

105. This paragraph best supports the statement that the police cannot search a person's home or private papers unless they have
   a. legal authorization.
   b. direct evidence of a crime.
   c. read the person his or her constitutional rights.
   d. a reasonable belief that a crime has occurred.
   e. requested that a judge be present.

Mathematics allows us to expand our consciousness. Mathematics tells us about economic trends, patterns of disease, and the growth of populations. Math is good at exposing the truth, but it can also perpetuate misunderstandings and untruths. Figures have the power to mislead people.

106. This paragraph best supports the statement that
   a. the study of mathematics is dangerous.
   b. words are more truthful than figures.
   c. the study of mathematics is more important than other disciplines.
   d. the power of numbers is that they cannot lie.
   e. figures are sometimes used to deceive people.

Human technology developed from the first stone tools about two and a half million years ago. In the beginning, the rate of development was slow. Hundreds of thousands of years passed without much change. Today, new technologies are reported daily on television and in newspapers.

107. This paragraph best supports the statement that
   a. stone tools were not really technology.
   b. stone tools were in use for two and a half million years.
   c. there is no way to know when stone tools first came into use.
   d. In today's world, new technologies are constantly being developed.
   e. none of the latest technologies are as significant as the development of stone tools.

Today's postal service is more efficient than ever. Mail that once took months to move by horse and foot now moves around the country in days or hours by truck, train, and plane. If your letter or package is urgent, the U.S. Postal Service offers Priority Mail and Express Mail services. Priority Mail is guaranteed to go anywhere in the United States in two days or less. Express Mail will get your package there overnight.

108. This paragraph best supports the statement that
   a. more people use the post office for urgent deliveries than any other delivery service.
   b. Express Mail is a good way to send urgent mail.
   c. Priority Mail usually takes two days or less.
   d. mail service today is more effective and dependable.
   e. mail was once delivered by horse and foot.

Reality TV shows will have an adverse effect on traditional dramas and comedies. As Reality TV increases in popularity, network executives will begin canceling more traditional programs and replacing them with the latest in Reality TV.

109. This paragraph best supports the statement that
   a. Reality TV is low quality.
   b. Reality TV shows get the highest ratings.
   c. more and more people love to watch and participate in Reality TV.
   d. as Reality TV gets more popular, more traditional television shows may be threatened.
   e. network executives make hasty and unwise decisions.

When writing business letters or memos, it's not practical to be personal. Though the first-person point of view may make the reader feel close to the writer, it also implies a certain subjectivity. That is, the writer is expressing a personal view from a personal perspective.

110. This paragraph best supports the statement that
   a. writing a first-person business correspondence will prevent the writer from getting promoted.
   b. effective business writing is one of the most important skills to have in an office environment.
   c. using the first-person point of view in business correspondence is not a wise choice.
   d. the first-person point of view expresses a personal view and a personal perspective.
   e. the first-person point of view is appropriate when writing a letter of thanks.

Topic Sentences

In the last section, you learned what a main idea is. Often, writers express their main idea in a clearly defined sentence known as a *topic sentence*. Topic sentences are usually found at the beginning of a paragraph in order to immediately establish the main idea. But this is not always the case—topic sentences can be found anywhere in a paragraph, and sometimes, the author chooses not to use one at all. Still, looking for the topic sentence is a good skill to have when ferreting out the meaning of a reading passage.

The answers to this section begin on page 135.

For the following three questions, choose the topic sentence that best fits the paragraph.

111. The term *spices* is a pleasant one, whether it connotes fine French cuisine or a down-home, cinnamon-flavored apple pie. _____. In the past, individuals traveled the world seeking exotic spices for profit and, in searching, have changed the course of history. Indeed, to gain control of lands harboring new spices, nations have actually gone to war.

   a. The taste and aroma of spices are the main elements that make food such a source of fascination and pleasure.

   b. The term might equally bring to mind Indian curry made thousands of miles away and those delicious barbecued ribs sold on the corner.

   c. It is exciting to find a good cookbook and experiment with spices from other lands—indeed, it is one way to travel around the globe!

   d. The history of spices, however, is another matter altogether, and at times, it can be filled with danger and intrigue.

112. It weighs less than three pounds and is hardly more interesting to look at than an overly ripe cauliflower. _____. It has created poetry and music, planned and executed horrific wars, and devised intricate scientific theories. It thinks and dreams, plots and schemes, and easily holds more information than all the libraries on Earth.

   a. The human brain is made of gelatinous matter and contains no nerve endings.

   b. The science of neurology has found a way to map the most important areas of the human brain.

   c. Nevertheless, the human brain is the most mysterious and complex object on Earth.

   d. However, scientists say that each person uses only 10% of his or her brain over the course of a lifetime!

113. Gary is a distinguished looking man with a touch of gray at the temples. Even in his early 50s, he still turns heads. He enjoys spending most of his time admiring his profile in the mirror. In fact, he considers his good looks to be his second-most important asset. The first, however, is money. He is lucky in this area, too, having been born into a wealthy family. _____. He loves the power his wealth has given him. He could buy whatever he desires, whether that be people, places, or things. Gary checks that mirror often and feels great delight with what he sees.

   a. Gary's gray hair is his worst characteristic.
   b. Conceit is the beginning and the end of Gary's character; conceit of person and situation.
   c. Gary feels blessed to be wealthy and the joy consumes his every thought.
   d. The only objects of Gary's respect are others who hold positions in society above him.

For the following questions, a topic sentence is given. Try choosing the sentence that best develops or supports it.

114. Life on Earth is ancient and, even at its first appearance, unimaginably complex.
   a. Scientists place its beginnings at some three billion years ago, when they hypothesize that the first molecule floated up out of the ooze with the unique ability to replicate itself.
   b. The most complex life form is, of course, the mammal—and the most complex mammal is humankind.
   c. It is unknown exactly where life started, where the first molecule was "born" that had the ability to replicate itself.
   d. Darwin's theory of evolution was one attempt to explain what essentially remains a great mystery.

115. Cosmetic plastic surgery is one of the fastest-growing segments of U.S. medicine.
   a. Cosmetic plastic surgery can have dangerous side effects, some of which can be fatal.
   b. Americans are eager to make their bodies as perfect as possible and to minimize the visible signs of aging.
   c. The price of cosmetic plastic surgery is also on the rise.
   d. This increase in cosmetic plastic surgery says something quite disturbing about our culture.

116. One scientific theory of the origin of the universe is the much misunderstood big bang theory.

   a. Physicists now believe they can construct what happened in the universe during the first three minutes of its beginning.

   b. Many scientists believe that, during microwave experiments, we can actually "hear" echoes of the big bang.

   c. The popular notion is that the big bang was a huge explosion in space, but this is far too simple a description.

   d. The big bang theory, if accepted, convinces us that the universe was not always as it is now.

117. Before we learn how to truly love someone else, we must learn how to love the face in the mirror.

   a. Don't be shy about meeting members of the opposite sex.

   b. No one can really love you the way you can love yourself.

   c. Love is not something that lasts unless one is very lucky.

   d. Learning to accept ourselves for who we are will teach us how to accept another person.

118. The Greek ideal of the hero most closely resembles today's free-agent superstar.

   a. A superstar is an athlete who commands a great salary based on his individual skills.

   b. The Greek warrior's focus was on grasping at immortality, and he did this by ensuring that his name would live on, long after he died.

   c. The Greek hero valued self-interest above loyalty to a cause, his king, or to his army, just as the free-agent superstar values his contract salary above any special team, coach, or the game.

   d. The Greek hero was impressive in his performance on the battlefield as well as in the sports arena.

119. There is no instruction by the old bird in the movements of flight; no conscious imitation by the young.

   a. The most obvious way in which birds differ from humans in behavior is that they can do all that they have to do, without ever being taught.

   b. More extraordinary than the fact that a bird is able to fly untaught, is that it is able to build a nest untaught.

   c. Young birds frequently make their first flights with their parents out of sight.

   d. Young birds brought up in artificial environments will build the proper kind of nest for their species when the time comes.

120. Parents play an important role in their children's academic success.

  a. Video games have a negative impact on children's academic success.

  b. Studies show that children of parents who regularly assist with homework and show an active interest in their child's studies bring home better grades.

  c. Studies show that watching less television and spending less time playing video games help children get better grades.

  d. Children who are avid readers get much better grades than their peers.

121. In special cases, needy people who have nowhere else to go are permitted to enter the United States as refugees.

  a. Other people, however, enter the United States illegally.

  b. The total number of newcomers was over one million.

  c. United States immigration laws put limits on the number of people permitted to enter the United States.

  d. As many as 12 million people may be living in the United States illegally.

122. The Puritans established a wide variety of punishments to enforce their strict laws.

  a. The Puritans believed that some lawbreakers should be shamed in public by the use of stocks and the pillory.

  b. Disobedient children would feel the sting of the whip.

  c. The Eighth Amendment of the Bill of Rights prohibits cruel and unusual punishment.

  d. Today, many of the punishments used by the Puritans seem cruel and excessive.

123. More and more people are eating organically grown fruits and vegetables.

  a. Organic food is usually more expensive than non-organic food.

  b. A wide variety of organic chocolate products are now available in stores.

  c. Raw foods are enjoying increasing popularity, now that people are discovering how a raw-foods diet leaves you feeling and looking great.

  d. Fresh organic produce contains more vitamins, minerals, and enzymes than non-organic produce.

124. In Oklahoma, a girl is forbidden to take a bite from her date's hamburger.

  a. It's illegal for teenagers to take a bath during the winter in Clinton, Indiana.

  b. Youngsters may not spin Yo-Yos on Sunday in Memphis, Tennessee.

  c. It may be hard to believe, but these types of strange laws are still on the books!

  d. It is illegal to parade an elephant down Main Street in Austin, Texas.

125. The hairs themselves are very sensitive.

  a. A cat's whiskers are among the most perfect organs of touch.

  b. The roots contain highly sensitive nerve endings.

  c. Serving as feelers, they aid the cat's ability to move in the dark.

  d. This is most important for a cat that does its prowling at night.

126. French explorers probably taught the Inuit Eskimos how to play dominoes.
   a. It was known in 181 A.D. in China.
   b. Also, it was played during the 1700s in Italy.
   c. The game of dominoes has been popular for centuries.
   d. From Italy, it was then introduced to the rest of the world.

127. People are now living longer than ever before for many different reasons.
   a. Some people in the Soviet Union's Caucasus Mountains live to be over 100 years of age.
   b. No one seems to understand this phenomenon.
   c. Advances in medical science have done wonders for longevity.
   d. The people in this region do not seem to gain anything from medical science.

128. For 16 years, he spread violence and death throughout the west.
   a. Jesse was gunned down on April 3, 1882.
   b. He left a trail of train and bank robberies.
   c. His crimes were committed during the late 1860s.
   d. Jesse Woodson James was the most legendary of all American outlaws.

For the final two questions, choose the sentence that does NOT support the given topic sentence.

129. In ancient Greece, honor was not just the domain of the warrior.
   a. A great orator [speaker], who could sway the public with his logic and wit, was greatly respected.
   b. A revered poet's name lived on long after he died.
   c. Great wealth was characteristic of the truly great kings.
   d. A warrior's quest for the esteem of his peers would bring him great prizes, which would secure a long-lasting reputation.

130. In *Moby Dick*, Herman Melville wrote that the whale men were "enveloped in whale lines," that each man relied on the others during moments of danger.
   a. The small boats that pursued the whales left the whaling ship far behind; each man in a boat had to depend on the others to stay alive.
   b. Once the whale was harpooned, the whale line unraveled so fast that water had to be poured on it to keep it from smoking.
   c. The whale line was the rope, dozens of yards long, that attached to the harpoon; it was raveled under the seats of all the men metaphorically connecting each man to the next.
   d. One wrong move and the line would snap a man right out of the boat; thus, his life depended on whether the crew would cut the whale loose to save him, or leave him in the ocean during the heat of the hunt.

Short Passages

In this section, you will find short (one and two paragraph) passages, accompanied by questions that ask you to identify explicit information, analyze, and interpret what is written. This is your first chance to use everything you've learned so far. Pay special attention to the details and the facts, and make a habit of trying to identify the author's main idea; also, try to think of the author's motive for writing the passage. As newspaper reporters do, ask the questions, "*Who? What? When? Where? How?* and *Why?*" Is the author's purpose to inform you of facts, persuade you of something, or simply to entertain you?

As you read, try marking up the passages or taking notes. The more active a reader you are, the more likely that you will understand and fully enjoy what you read.

The answers to this section begin on page 137.

Some of the questions following the passages ask you to make *inferences* from the passages. To *infer* means to arrive at a conclusion by reasoning from evidence. Synonyms for *infer* are *deduce, judge,* or *conclude.* If you are told to *infer* something from a passage, you are basically being asked what conclusions can be drawn from the content of the story. Tip: If you replace the word *infer* with *conclude* in a question, it may make more sense to you.

In cities throughout the country, there is a new direction in local campaign coverage. Frequently in local elections, journalists are not giving voters enough information to understand the issues and evaluate the candidates. The local news media devotes too much time to scandal and not enough time to policy.

131. This paragraph best supports the statement that the local news media

a. is not doing an adequate job when it comes to covering local campaigns.

b. does not understand either campaign issues or politics.

c. should learn how to cover politics by watching the national news media.

d. has no interest in covering stories about local political events.

The use of desktop computer equipment and software to create high-quality documents such as newsletters, business cards, letterhead, and brochures is called Desktop Publishing, or DTP. The most important part of any DTP project is planning. Before you begin, you should know your intended audience, the message you want to communicate, and what form your message will take.

132. The paragraph best supports the statement that

a. Desktop Publishing is one way to become acquainted with a new business audience.

b. computer software is continually being refined to produce high-quality printing.

c. the first stage of any proposed DTP project should be organization and design.

d. the planning stage of any DTP project should include talking with the intended audience.

The entire low-carbohydrate versus low-fat diet argument is so prevalent that one would think that these are the only two options available for losing weight and staying healthy. Some experts even feel that the low-carb/low-fat debate distracts us from an even more important issue—our culture's reliance on processed and manufactured foods.

133. The paragraph best supports the statement that

a. experts state that not all fats are equal, so we need not reduce our intake of all fats; just those that contain partially hydrogenated oils.

b. important health concerns get overlooked when we focus exclusively on the low-fat versus low-carb question.

c. low-carbohydrate diets lead to significant and sustained weight loss.

d. processed foods can lead to many adverse health problems including heart disease, cancer, diabetes, and obesity.

Every year, Americans use over one billion sharp objects to administer healthcare in their homes. These sharp objects include lancets, needles, and syringes. If not disposed of in puncture-resistant containers, they can injure sanitation workers. Sharp objects should be disposed of in hard plastic or metal containers with secure lids. The containers should be clearly marked and be puncture resistant.

134. The paragraph best supports the idea that sanitation workers can be injured if they
   a. do not place sharp objects in puncture-resistant containers.
   b. come in contact with sharp objects that have not been placed in secure containers.
   c. are careless with sharp objects such as lancets, needles, and syringes in their homes.
   d. do not mark the containers they pick up with a warning that those containers contain sharp objects.

Litigation is not always the only or best way to resolve conflicts. Mediation offers an alternative approach and it is one that can be quite efficient and successful. Mediation can be faster, less expensive, and can lead to creative solutions not always possible in a court of law. Additionally, mediation focuses on mutually acceptable solutions, rather than on winning or losing.

135. This paragraph best supports the idea that
   a. there is too much reliance on litigation in our society.
   b. litigation is expensive, slow, and limited by its reliance on following the letter of the law.
   c. mediation is the best way to resolve a crisis.
   d. mediation can be an effective way to resolve conflicts.

One of the missions of the Peace Corps is to help the people of interested countries meet their need for trained men and women. People who work for the Peace Corps do so because they want to, but to keep the agency dynamic with fresh ideas, no staff member can work for the agency for more than five years.

136. The paragraph best supports the statement that Peace Corps employees
   a. are highly intelligent people.
   b. must train for about five years.
   c. are hired for a limited term of employment.
   d. have both academic and work experience.

More and more office workers telecommute from offices in their own homes. The upside of tele-commuting is both greater productivity and greater flexibility. Telecommuters produce, on average, 20% more than if they were to work in an office, and their flexible schedule allows them to balance both their family and work responsibilities.

137. The paragraph best supports the statement that telecommuters
   a. get more work done in a given time period than workers who travel to the office.
   b. produce a better quality work product than workers who travel to the office.
   c. are more flexible in their ideas than workers who travel to the office.
   d. would do 20% more work if they were to work in an office.

Sushi, the thousand-year-old Japanese delicacy, started small in the United States, in a handful of restaurants in big cities. Today, sushi consumption in America is 50% greater than it was ten years ago and not just in restaurants. Sushi is also sold at concession stands in sports stadiums, university dining halls, and in supermarkets throughout the country.

138. This paragraph best supports the statement that
   a. sushi is now a fast food as popular as hot dogs, burgers, and fries.
   b. more sushi is sold in restaurants than in supermarkets.
   c. Americans are more adventurous eaters than they were in the past.
   d. sushi wasn't always widely available in the United States.

Today's shopping mall has as its antecedents historical marketplaces, such as Greek *agoras*, European *piazzas*, and Asian *bazaars*. The purpose of these sites, as with the shopping mall, is both economic and social. People not only go to buy and sell wares, but also to be seen, catch up on news, and be part of the human drama.

139. The paragraph best supports the statement that
   a. modern Americans spend an average of 15 hours a month in shopping malls.
   b. shopping malls serve an important purpose in our culture.
   c. shopping malls have a social as well as commercial function.
   d. there are historical antecedents for almost everything in contemporary society.

Daffodil bulbs require well-drained soil and a sunny planting location. They should be planted in holes that are 3–6 inches deep and there should be 2–4 inches between bulbs. The bulb should be placed in the hole, pointed side up, root side down. Once the bulb is planted, water the area thoroughly.

140. According to the above directions, when planting daffodil bulbs, which of the following conditions is not necessary?
   a. a sunny location
   b. well-drained soil
   c. proper placement of bulbs in soil
   d. proper fertilization

141. According to the above directions, which of the following is true?
   a. Daffodils do best in sandy soil.
   b. Daffodil bulbs should be planted in autumn for spring blooming.
   c. It is possible to plant daffodil bulbs upside down.
   d. Daffodil bulbs require daily watering.

Many cities haves distributed standardized recycling containers to all households with directions that read: "We would prefer that you use this new container as your primary recycling container as this will expedite pick-up of recyclables. Additional recycling containers may be purchased from the City."

142. According to the directions, each household
   a. may only use one recycling container.
   b. must use the new recycling container.
   c. should use the new recycling container.
   d. must buy a new recycling container.

143. According to the directions, which of the following is true about the new containers?

    a. The new containers are far better than other containers in every way.

    b. The new containers will help increase the efficiency of the recycling program.

    c. The new containers hold more than the old containers did.

    d. The new containers are less expensive than the old containers.

Ratatouille is a dish that has grown in popularity over the last few years. It features eggplant, zucchini, tomatoes, peppers, and garlic; chopped, mixed, sautéed, and finally, cooked slowly over low heat. As the vegetables cook slowly, they make their own broth, which may be extended with a little tomato paste. The name *ratatouille* comes from the French word *touiller*, meaning to stir or mix together.

144. Which of the following is the correct order of steps for making ratatouille?

    a. chop vegetables, add tomato paste, stir or mix together

    b. mix the vegetables together, sauté them, and add tomato paste

    c. cook the vegetables slowly, mix them together, add tomato paste

    d. add tomato paste to extend the broth and cook slowly over low heat

145. Ratatouille can best be described as a

    a. French pastry.

    b. sauce to put over vegetables.

    c. pasta dish extended with tomato paste.

    d. vegetable stew.

The competitive civil-service system is designed to give candidates fair and equal treatment and to ensure that federal applicants are hired based on objective criteria. Hiring has to be based solely on a candidate's knowledge, skills, and abilities (which you'll sometimes see abbreviated as *ksa*), and not on external factors such as race, religion, sex, and so on. Whereas employers in the private sector can hire employees for subjective reasons, federal employers must be able to justify their decision with objective evidence that the candidate is qualified.

146. The paragraph best supports the statement that

    a. hiring in the private sector is inherently unfair.

    b. *ksa* is not as important as test scores to federal employers.

    c. federal hiring practices are simpler than those employed by the private sector.

    d. the civil service strives to hire on the basis of a candidate's abilities.

147. The federal government's practice of hiring on the basis of *ksa* frequently results in the hiring of employees

    a. based on race, religion, sex, and so forth.

    b. who are unqualified for the job.

    c. who are qualified for the job.

    d. on the basis of subjective judgment.

It is well known that the world urgently needs adequate distribution of food, so that everyone gets enough. Adequate distribution of medicine is just as urgent. Medical expertise and medical supplies need to be redistributed throughout the world so that people in emerging nations will have proper medical care.

148. This paragraph best supports the statement that
- **a.** the majority of the people in the world have no medical care.
- **b.** medical resources in emerging nations have diminished in the past few years.
- **c.** not enough doctors give time and money to those in need of medical care.
- **d.** many people who live in emerging nations are not receiving proper medical care.

Knitting has made a major comeback. People are knitting on college campuses, in coffee shops, and in small knitting groups throughout the United States. New knitting stores, many with cafes, are popping up all over, and there are more knitting books and magazines being published than ever before. And not all of these knitters are women: As knitting continues to surge in popularity, men are picking up knitting needles in record numbers.

149. The paragraph best supports the statement that
- **a.** joining a knitting group is a great way to make new friends.
- **b.** some people knit because it helps them relax and release stress.
- **c.** today's knitter is not the stereotypical grandmother in a rocking chair.
- **d.** as is the case with all fads, this new obsession with knitting will fade quickly.

Everyone is sensitive to extreme weather conditions. But with age, the body may become less able to respond to long exposure to very hot or very cold temperatures. Some older people might develop hypothermia when exposed to cold weather. Hypothermia is a drop in internal body temperature, which can be fatal if not detected and treated.

150. The paragraph best supports the statement that
- **a.** cold weather is more dangerous for older people than warm weather.
- **b.** hypothermia is a condition that only affects older people.
- **c.** older people who live in warm climates are healthier than older people who live in cold climates.
- **d.** an older person is more susceptible to hypothermia than a younger person.

Whether you can accomplish a specific goal or meet a specific deadline depends first on how much time you need to get the job done. What should you do when the demands of the job exceed the time you have available? The best approach is to divide the project into smaller pieces. Different goals will have to be divided in different ways, but one seemingly unrealistic goal can often be accomplished by working on several smaller, more reasonable goals.

151. The main idea of the passage is that
- **a.** jobs often remain only partially completed because of lack of time.
- **b.** the best way to complete projects is to make sure your goals are achievable.
- **c.** the best way to tackle a large project is to separate it into smaller parts.
- **d.** the best approach to a demanding job is to delegate responsibility.

Health clubs have undergone a major transformation that can be described in three words: mind, body, and spirit. Loud, fast, heart-thumping aerobics has been replaced by the hushed tones of yoga and the controlled movements of Pilates. The clubs are responding to the needs of their customers who are increasingly looking for a retreat from their hectic lifestyles and a way to find a healthy balance in their lives by nurturing their whole selves.

152. The main idea of the paragraph is that
- **a.** exercise is less important now than it once was.
- **b.** health clubs are much less popular now than they were ten years ago.
- **c.** many health clubs will go out of business because of the decline in traditional exercise.
- **d.** people's desire to nurture all aspects of themselves has contributed to big changes for health clubs.

For most judges, sentencing a person who has been convicted of a crime is a difficult decision. In the majority of jurisdictions throughout the country, judges have few sentencing options from which to choose. Generally, their options are confined to a fine, probation, or incarceration. Crimes, however, cover a wide spectrum of criminal behavior and motivation, and a wide variety of sanctions should be available.

153. The main idea of the paragraph is that
- **a.** there should be laws that dictate which sentence a judge should hand down.
- **b.** someone other than a judge should be allowed to sentence a criminal.
- **c.** judges should be given more sentencing options from which to choose.
- **d.** more money should be spent on the criminal justice system.

Before you begin to compose a business letter, sit down and think about your purpose in writing the letter. Do you want to request information, order a product, register a complaint, or apply for something? Do some brainstorming and gather information before you begin writing. Always keep your objective in mind.

154. The main idea of the passage is that
- **a.** planning is an important part of writing a business letter.
- **b.** business letters are frequently complaint letters.
- **c.** brainstorming and writing take approximately equal amounts of time.
- **d.** many people fail to plan ahead when they are writing a business letter.

Keeping busy at important tasks is much more motivating than having too little to do. Today's employees are not afraid of responsibility. Most people are willing to take on extra responsibility in order to have more variety in their positions. In addition, along with that responsibility should come more authority to independently carry out some important tasks.

155. The main idea of the paragraph is that
- **a.** variety and independence on the job increase employee motivation.
- **b.** to avoid boredom, many people do more work than their jobs require of them.
- **c.** today's employees are demanding more independence than ever before.
- **d.** office jobs in the past have carried less responsibility.

Managing job and family is not simple. Both commitments make strong demands on people and are sometimes in direct opposition to each other. Saying yes to one means saying no to the other, and stress can often result. Being realistic and creating a balance in life can help set priorities.

156. The main idea of the paragraph is that
   a. most family responsibilities cause stress at home and at work.
   b. because it pays the bills, a job must take priority over other commitments.
   c. it is important to have a balance between job and family responsibilities.
   d. because they are so important, family duties must take priority over the job.

Women business owners are critically important to the American economy, yet women still face unique obstacles in the business world. The U.S. Small Business Administration offers a variety of programs and services to help women-owned businesses succeed and to advocate for women entrepreneurs.

157. This paragraph best supports the statement that women business owners
   a. have more success in the United States than in other countries.
   b. cannot succeed without outside help.
   c. may find the Small Business Administration a useful resource.
   d. should not make any major decisions without seeking the advice of the Small Business Administration.

Passages in this section can have one to six questions following. You must respond accordingly.

Use of electronic mail (e-mail) has been widespread for more than a decade. E-mail simplifies the flow of ideas, connects people from distant offices, eliminates the need for meetings, and often boosts productivity. However, e-mail should be carefully managed to avoid unclear and inappropriate communication. E-mail messages should be concise and limited to one topic. When complex issues need to be addressed, phone calls are still best.

158. The main idea of the paragraph is that e-mail
   a. is not always the easiest way to connect people from distant offices.
   b. has changed considerably since it first began a decade ago.
   c. causes people to be unproductive when it is used incorrectly.
   d. is effective for certain kinds of messages but only if managed wisely.

159. Which of the following would be the most appropriate title for the passage?
   a. Appropriate Use of E-Mail
   b. E-Mail's Popularity
   c. E-Mail: The Ideal Form of Communication
   d. Why Phone Calls Are Better Than E-Mail

Native American art often incorporates a language of abstract visual symbols. The artist gives a poetic message to the viewer, communicating the beauty of an idea, either by using religious symbols or a design from nature such as rain on leaves or sunshine on water. The idea communicated may even be purely whimsical, in which case the artist might start out with symbols developed from a bird's tracks or a child's toy.

160. The main idea of the passage is that Native American art
   a. is purely poetic and dreamlike.
   b. is usually abstract, although it can also be poetic and beautiful.
   c. communicates the beauty of ideas through the use of symbols.
   d. is sometimes purely whimsical.

In criminal cases, the availability of readable fingerprints is often critical in establishing evidence of a major crime. It is necessary, therefore, to follow proper procedures when taking fingerprints. In major cases, prints should be obtained from all persons who may have touched areas associated with a crime scene, for elimination purposes.

161. The main idea of the paragraph is that
   a. because fingerprints are so important in many cases, it is important to follow the correct course in taking them.
   b. all fingerprints found at a crime scene should be taken and thoroughly investigated.
   c. if the incorrect procedure is followed in gathering fingerprints, the ones taken may be useless.
   d. the first step in investigating fingerprints is to eliminate those of non-suspects.

162. The paragraph best supports the statement that
   a. no crimes can be solved without readable fingerprints.
   b. all persons who have touched an area in a crime scene are suspects.
   c. all fingerprints found at a crime scene are used in court as evidence.
   d. all persons who have touched a crime-scene area should be fingerprinted.

An ecosystem is a group of animals and plants living in a specific region and interacting with one another and with their physical environment. Ecosystems include physical and chemical components, such as soils, water, and nutrients that support the organisms living there. These organisms may range from large animals to microscopic bacteria. Ecosystems also can be thought of as the interactions among all organisms in a given habitat; for instance, one species may serve as food for another. People are part of the ecosystems where they live and work. Human activities can harm or destroy local ecosystems unless actions such as land development for housing or businesses are carefully planned to conserve and sustain the ecology of the area. An important part of ecosystem management involves finding ways to protect and enhance economic and social well-being while protecting local ecosystems.

163. What is the main idea of the passage?

   a. An ecosystem is a community that includes animals, plants, and microscopic bacteria.

   b. Human activities can do great damage to local ecosystems, so human communities should be cautiously planned.

   c. In managing the ecology of an area, it is important to protect both human interests and the interests of other members of local ecosystems.

   d. People should remember that they are a part of the ecosystems where they live and work.

164. Which of the following best sums up activities within an ecosystem?

   a. predator-prey relationships

   b. interactions among all members

   c. human-animal interactions

   d. human relationship with the environment

165. An ecosystem can most accurately be defined as a

   a. geographical area.

   b. community.

   c. habitat.

   d. protected environment.

Once people wore garlic around their necks to ward off disease. Today, most Americans would scoff at the idea of wearing a necklace of garlic cloves to enhance their well-being. However, you might find a number of Americans willing to ingest capsules of pulverized garlic or other herbal supplements in the name of health.

Complementary and alternative medicine, which includes a range of practices outside of conventional medicine such as herbs, homeopathy, massage therapy, yoga, and acupuncture, hold increasing appeal for Americans. In fact, according to one estimate, 42% of Americans have used alternative therapies. In all age groups, the use of unconventional healthcare practices has steadily increased in the last 30 years, and the trend is likely to continue, although people born before 1945 are the least likely to turn to these therapies.

Why have so many patients turned to alternative therapies? Many are frustrated by the time constraints of managed care and alienated by conventional medicine's focus on technology. Others feel that a holistic approach to healthcare better reflects their beliefs and values. Others seek therapies that relieve symptoms associated with chronic disease; symptoms that mainstream medicine cannot treat.

Some alternative therapies have even crossed the line into mainstream medicine, as scientific investigation has confirmed their safety and efficacy. For example, physicians may currently prescribe acupuncture for pain management or to control the nausea associated with chemotherapy. Additionally, many U.S. medical schools teach courses in alternative therapies, and many health insurance companies offer some alternative medicine benefits.

166. What is the main idea of this passage?
   a. Alternative medicine is now a big business in the United States with more Americans seeking it out than ever before.
   b. Today, it is not unusual for mainstream doctors to incorporate alternative therapies into their practice.
   c. Over the last few decades, alternative medicine has become more popular, accepted, and practiced in the United States.
   d. People are tired of conventional medicine's focus on technology.

167. According to the passage, which practice would not be defined as alternative medicine?
   a. pain management
   b. acupuncture
   c. taking herbal garlic supplements
   d. massage therapy

168. Based on the information given, what kind of person would be least likely to seek out alternative medical treatment?
   a. a senior citizen suffering from chemotherapy-induced nausea
   b. a young woman suffering from chronic fatigue syndrome
   c. a 45-year-old man who believes that his body and mind must be treated together.
   d. a 25-year-old track star with chronic back pain

169. The passage indicates that alternative treatments are increasingly being used by mainstream medical professionals because
   a. more and more Americans are demanding alternative therapies.
   b. healthcare insurance companies are now providing some benefits for alternative medical treatments.
   c. they are frustrated by the time constraints of managed care.
   d. scientific studies are becoming available that prove their effectiveness and safety.

On February 3, 1956, Autherine Lucy became the first African-American student to attend the University of Alabama, although the dean of women refused to allow Autherine to live in a university dormitory. White students rioted in protest of her admission, and the federal government had to assume command of the Alabama National Guard in order to protect her. Nonetheless, on her first day in class, Autherine bravely took a seat in the front row. She remembers being surprised that the professor of the class appeared not to notice she was even in class. Later, she would appreciate his seeming indifference, as he was one of only a few professors to speak out in favor of her right to attend the university.

For protection, Autherine was taken in and out of classroom buildings by the back door and driven from class to class by an assistant to the university president. The students continued to riot, and one day, the windshield of the car she was in was broken. University officials suspended her, saying it was for her own safety. When her attorney issued a statement in her name protesting her suspension, the university used it as grounds for expelling her for insubordination. Although she never finished her education at the University of Alabama, Autherine Lucy's courage was an inspiration to African-American students who followed her lead and desegregated universities all over the United States.

170. According to the passage, what did Autherine Lucy do on her first day at the University of Alabama?
   a. She moved into a dormitory.
   b. She sat in the front row of her class.
   c. She became terrified of the white rioters.
   d. She was befriended by an assistant to the university president.

171. Based on the information in the passage, which of the following best describes Autherine Lucy?
   a. quiet and shy
   b. courageous and determined
   c. clever and amusing
   d. overly dramatic

172. When she began classes at the university, Autherine Lucy expected to
   a. stand out from the other students.
   b. have the support of the university faculty.
   c. join an African-American organization for protection.
   d. be ridiculed by the professors.

173. Autherine Lucy never graduated from the University of Alabama because she
   a. moved to another state.
   b. transferred to another university.
   c. dropped out because of pressure from other students.
   d. was expelled for insubordination.

174. According to the passage, which of the following is true?
   a. The Alabama National Guard is normally under the command of the U.S. Army.
   b. In 1956, the only segregated university in the United States was in Alabama.
   c. Autherine Lucy was escorted to and from class by the university president's assistant.
   d. A few white students at the university were pleased that Autherine Lucy was a student there.

Kwanzaa is a holiday celebrated by many African Americans from December 26 to January 1. It pays tribute to the rich cultural roots of Americans of African ancestry, and celebrates family, community, and culture. Kwanzaa means *the first* or *the first fruits of the harvest* and is based on the ancient African first-fruit harvest celebrations. The modern holiday of Kwanzaa was founded in 1966 by Dr. Maulana Karenga, a professor at the California State University in Long Beach, California. The seven-day celebration encourages people to think about their African roots as well as their life in present-day America.

The seven fundamental principles on which Kwanzaa is based are referred to as the *Nguzo Saba*. These rules consist of unity, self-determination, collective work and responsibility, cooperative economics, purpose, creativity, and faith. Participants celebrate by performing rituals such as lighting the kinara. The kinara is symbolic of the continental Africans. Each of its seven candles represents a distinct principle beginning with unity, the black center candle. Talking with family, drumming, singing, and dancing are all part of the celebration activities.

175. According to the passage, the holiday of Kwanzaa was created in order to
   a. celebrate African Americans' harvesting skills.
   b. honor Dr. Maulana Karenga.
   c. encourage African Americans to think about their roots.
   d. light the individual candles of the kinara.

176. Which of the seven principles does the black center candle of the kinara represent?
   a. unity
   b. faith
   c. creativity
   d. responsibility

177. According to the passage, Kwanzaa is celebrated by all of the following EXCEPT
   a. drumming and rituals.
   b. dancing and singing.
   c. dialogue.
   d. solitude and silence.

178. Which of the following is the best definition of Kwanzaa?
   a. the first song of the month
   b. the first corn of the harvest
   c. the first dance of the night
   d. the first fruits of the harvest

In 1519, Hernando Cortez led his army of Spanish Conquistadors into Mexico. Equipped with horses, shining armor, and the most advanced weapons of the sixteenth century, he fought his way from the flat coastal area into the mountainous highlands. Cortez was looking for gold, and he was sure that Indian groups in Mexico had mined large amounts of the precious metal. First, he conquered the groups and then seized their precious gold. His methods were very organized.

Initially, Cortez defeated the Tlascalans, and then formed an alliance with them to defeat the Aztecs, their enemies. Because of an Aztec prophecy about the return of Quetzacoatl, a legendary god-king who was light skinned and bearded, Cortez was believed to be a god and was received by the Aztecs with honor. Later, this warm welcome turned to mistrust and hatred when the Spaniards mistreated the Aztec people. Eventually, the Aztec capital, Tenochtitlan, fell to the Spaniards. Cortez had Tenochtitlan razed and built Mexico City on its ruins.

179. According to the passage, which one of the following did NOT cause the defeat of the Aztecs?
- **a.** The Aztecs initially thought that Cortez was a god.
- **b.** Cortez knew how to form alliances with the Aztecs' enemies.
- **c.** The Conquistadors had advanced weapons.
- **d.** The Spanish outnumbered the Aztecs.

180. The reader can infer from the passage that the Aztecs thought Cortez was the god from their prophecy because
- **a.** he was light skinned and had a beard.
- **b.** he rode a magnificent horse.
- **c.** he spoke a foreign language.
- **d.** he offered friendship.

181. According to the passage, what was Cortez's major goal in his exploits?
- **a.** to befriend the Aztecs
- **b.** to get married
- **c.** to return to Spain
- **d.** to gain wealth and power

182. Which of the following sayings should the Aztecs have heeded?
- **a.** Seeing is believing.
- **b.** Beware of strangers.
- **c.** There's no place like home.
- **d.** A friend in need is a friend indeed.

Theodore Roosevelt was born with asthma and poor eyesight, yet this sickly child later won fame as a political leader, a Rough Rider, and a hero of the common people. To conquer his handicaps, Teddy trained in a gym and became a lightweight boxer at Harvard. Out west, he hunted buffalo and ran a cattle ranch. Back east, he became a civil service reformer and police commissioner. He became President McKinley's assistant Navy secretary during the Spanish-American War. Also, he led a charge of cavalry Rough Riders up San Juan Hill in Cuba. After achieving fame, he became governor of New York and went on to become the vice president.

When McKinley was assassinated, Theodore Roosevelt became the youngest president at age 42. He is famous for his motto, "Speak softly and carry a big stick." Roosevelt battled for meat inspection and pure-food laws. Also, he wanted to save the forests and break the grip that big business had on steel and oil. Roosevelt persuaded the diplomats of warring Russia and Japan to make peace.

183. Which of the following states the main idea of the passage?
   a. Theodore Roosevelt was a man of many accomplishments.
   b. Presidents should speak softly and carry big sticks.
   c. Presidents can help countries make peace.
   d. A governor can become a president.

184. What achievement illustrates Roosevelt's ability to overcome personal obstacles?
   a. He led a charge of cavalry Rough Riders in Cuba.
   b. He is famous for his motto, "Speak softly and carry a big stick."
   c. He overcame his asthma by training in a gym, and he became a boxer.
   d. He became governor of New York.

185. According to the passage, how did Roosevelt first become president?
   a. He won the support of his party in a political campaign.
   b. As vice president, he took over the presidency when McKinley was assassinated.
   c. He won the nation's popular vote.
   d. He won the necessary Electoral College votes.

186. He first worked under President McKinley in what capacity?
   a. assistant Navy secretary during the Spanish-American War
   b. police commissioner
   c. governor of New York
   d. civil service reformer

Charles Darwin was born in 1809 in Shrewsbury, England. He was a biologist whose famous theory of evolution is important to philosophy for the effect it has had on ideas relating to the nature of men. After many years of careful study, Darwin attempted to show that higher species came into existence as a result of the gradual transformation of lower species, and that the process of transformation could be explained through the selective effect of the natural environment upon organisms. He concluded that the principles of *natural selection* and *survival of the fittest* govern all life. Darwin's explanation of these principles is that because of the food supply problem, the young of any species compete for survival. Those young that survive to produce the next generation tend to embody favorable natural changes that are passed on by heredity. His major work that contained these theories is *On the Origin of the Species,* written in 1859. Many religious opponents condemned this work.

187. According to the passage, Charles Darwin was which of the following?
   a. a priest
   b. a biologist
   c. an animal trainer
   d. a politician

188. Which of the following statements supports Darwin's belief about the origin of all species?
   a. Man is descended from monkeys.
   b. All life forms developed slowly over time from lower life forms.
   c. Natural forces do not affect life on Earth.
   d. All species were individually created.

189. Darwin's explanation that the young of any species compete for food and survival, and those that survive are strong and pass their traits on to their young was called which of the following?
  a. belief in creationism
  b. the catastrophic theory
  c. theory of natural selection and survival of the fittest
  d. the study of anthropology

190. According to the passage, how was Darwin's book, *On the Origin of the Species*, received?
  a. Scientists gave their immediate approval of Darwin's book.
  b. Religious opponents condemned Darwin's book.
  c. The world ignored Darwin's book.
  d. Darwin's book became an immediate bestseller.

The crystal clear, blue water and the magnificent sun make the Caribbean island of Saint Maarten a favorite vacation spot, one that is popular with North Americans during their winter holidays from December through March, as well as with South Americans and Europeans from April through August. The French and Dutch settled on the island in the 1600s, and to this day, the island is divided between the two of them. The French capital is Marigot; the Dutch capital is Philipsburg.

Tourists soon discover that St. Maarten has an intriguing history. Ancient artifacts found on the island date back to the Stone Age, 6,000 years ago! Tourists also learn that 1,200 years ago the Arawak Indians inhabited all the islands of the West Indies and were a peaceful people living under the guidance of their chiefs. Three hundred years after the Arawaks first arrived on St.

Maarten, in the 1300s, they were defeated and forced to abandon the island by a hostile tribe of Indians originating in South America. This new tribe was called the Carib. The Caribbean Sea was named after them. Unlike the Arawaks, they had no permanent chiefs or leaders, except in times of <u>strife</u>. And they were extremely warlike. Worse, they were cannibalistic, eating the enemy warriors they captured. In fact, the very word *cannibal* comes from the Spanish name for the Carib Indians. The Spanish arrived in the fifteenth century and, unfortunately, they carried diseases to which the Indians had no immunity. Many Indians succumbed to common European illnesses; others died from the hard labor forced upon them.

191. One can infer from the passage that the Stone Age people lived on St. Maarten around the year
  a. 6000 B.C.
  b. 4000 B.C.
  c. 800 A.D.
  d. 1300 A.D.

192. Which of the following is NOT true about the Carib Indians?
  a. The sea was named after them.
  b. They were peaceful fishermen, hunters, and farmers.
  c. They ate human flesh.
  d. They settled after defeating the Arawak Indians.

193. According to the passage, the Carib Indians were finally defeated by
  a. sickness and forced labor.
  b. the more aggressive Arawak tribe.
  c. the Dutch West India Company.
  d. the French explorers.

194. One can infer from the passage that the underlined word *strife* means
a. cannibalism.
b. war.
c. duty-free.
d. chief.

195. According to the article, present-day St. Maarten
a. belongs to the Spanish.
b. is independent.
c. is shared by the French and the Dutch.
d. is part of the U.S. Virgin Islands.

A metaphor is a poetic device that deals with comparison. It compares similar qualities of two dissimilar objects. With a simple metaphor, one object becomes the other: *Love is a rose.* Although this does not sound like a particularly rich image, a metaphor can communicate so much about a particular image that poets use them more than any other type of figurative language. The reason for this is that poets compose their poetry to express what they are experiencing emotionally at that moment. Consequently, what the poet imagines love to be may or may not be our perception of love. Therefore, the poet's job is to enable us to *experience* it, to feel it the same way that the poet does. We should be able to nod in agreement and say, "Yes, that's it! I understand precisely where this person is coming from."

Let's analyze this remarkably unsophisticated metaphor concerning love and the rose to see what it offers. Because the poet uses a comparison with a rose, first we must examine the characteristics of that flower. A rose is spectacular in its beauty, its petals are velvety soft, and its aroma is soothing and pleasing. It's possible to say that a rose is actually a veritable feast to the senses: the visual, the tactile, and the aural [more commonly known as the senses of sight, touch, and sound]. The rose's appearance seems to border on perfection, each petal seemingly symmetrical in form. Isn't this the way one's love should be? A loved one should be a delight to one's senses and seem perfect. However, there is another dimension added to the comparison by using a rose. Roses have thorns. This is the comprehensive image the poet wants to communicate; otherwise, a daisy or a mum would have been presented to the audience as the ultimate representation of love—but the poet didn't, instead conveying the idea that roses can be treacherous. So can love, the metaphor tells us. When one reaches out with absolute trust to touch the object of his or her affection, ouch, a thorn can cause great harm! "Be careful," the metaphor admonishes: Love is a feast to the senses, but it can overwhelm us, and it can also hurt us. It can prick us and cause acute suffering. This is the poet's perception of love—an admonition. What is the point? Just this: It took almost 14 sentences to clarify what a simple metaphor communicates in only five words! *That* is the artistry and the joy of the simple metaphor.

196. The main idea of this passage is
a. poetic devices are necessary for poets.
b. poetry must never cater to the senses.
c. always use words that create one specific image.
d. the metaphor is a great poetic device.

197. It can be inferred that a metaphor is
a. a type of figurative language.
b. the only poetic device.
c. not precise enough.
d. a type of flower in a poem.

198. According to the passage, thorns
   a. protect the rose from harm.
   b. reduce the ability to love another.
   c. add a new element to the image of love.
   d. are just more images to compare to a rose.

199. It can be inferred that the true meaning of the *love is a rose* metaphor is that
   a. love is a true joy.
   b. love comes only once in a lifetime.
   c. love is never permanent.
   d. love is a combination of good and bad experiences.

200. According to the passage, the poet's intention is
   a. to release anger.
   b. to announce heartache.
   c. to enable you to experience the poet's point of view.
   d. to reward the senses.

The composer Wolfgang Amadeus Mozart's remarkable musical talent was apparent even before most children can sing a simple nursery rhyme. Wolfgang's older sister Maria Anna (who the family called Nannerl) was learning the clavier, an early keyboard instrument, when her three-year-old brother took an interest in playing. As Nannerl later recalled, Wolfgang "often spent much time at the clavier picking out thirds, which he was always striking, and his pleasure showed that it sounded good." Their father Leopold, an assistant concertmaster at the Salzburg Court, recognized his children's unique gifts and soon devoted himself to their musical education.

Born in Salzburg, Austria, on January 27, 1756, Wolfgang had composed his first original work by age five. Leopold planned to take Nannerl and Wolfgang on tour to play before the European courts. Their first venture was to nearby Munich where the children played for Maximillian III Joseph, elector of Bavaria. Leopold soon set his sights on the capital of the Hapsburg Empire, Vienna. On their way to Vienna, the family stopped in Linz, where Wolfgang gave his first public concert. By this time, Wolfgang was not only a virtuoso harpsichord player, but he had also mastered the violin. The audience at Linz was stunned by the six-year-old, and word of his genius soon traveled to Vienna. In a much anticipated concert, the Mozart children appeared at the Schonbrunn Palace on October 13, 1762. They utterly charmed the emperor and empress.

Following this success, Leopold was inundated with invitations for the children to play, for a fee. Leopold seized the opportunity and booked as many concerts as possible at courts throughout Europe. A concert could last three hours, and the children played at least two per a day. Today, Leopold might be considered the worst kind of stage parent, but at the time, it was not uncommon for prodigies to make extensive concert tours. Even so, it was an exhausting schedule for a child who was just past the age of needing an afternoon nap.

201. A good title for this passage would be
   a. Classical Music in the Eighteenth Century: An Overview.
   b. Stage Parents: A Historical Perspective.
   c. Mozart: The Early Life of a Musical Prodigy.
   d. Mozart: The Short Career of a Musical Genius.

202. According to the passage, Wolfgang became interested in music because
   a. his father thought it would be profitable.
   b. he had a natural talent.
   c. he saw his sister learning to play an instrument.
   d. he came from a musical family.

203. What was the consequence of Wolfgang's first public appearance?
   a. He charmed the emperor and empress of Hapsburg.
   b. Word of Wolfgang's genius spread to the capital.
   c. Leopold set his sights on Vienna.
   d. Invitations for the miracle children to play poured in.

204. Each of the following statements about Wolfgang Mozart is directly supported by the passage EXCEPT
   a. Mozart's father, Leopold, was instrumental in shaping his career.
   b. Maria Anna was a talented musician in her own right.
   c. Wolfgang's childhood was devoted to his musical career.
   d. Wolfgang preferred the violin to other instruments.

205. According to the passage, during Wolfgang's early years, child prodigies were
   a. few and far between.
   b. accustomed to extensive concert tours.
   c. expected to spend at least six hours per day practicing their music.
   d. expected to play for courts throughout Europe.

206. Based on information found in the passage, Mozart can best be described as
   a. a child prodigy.
   b. a workaholic.
   c. the greatest composer of the eighteenth century.
   d. a victim of his father's ambition.

The sentences are numbered in the following passage to help you answer the questions.

1) The Woodstock Music and Art Fair—better known to its participants and to history simply as "Woodstock"—should have been a colossal failure. 2) Just a month prior to its August 15, 1969 opening, the fair's organizers were informed by the council of Wallkill, New York, that permission to hold the festival was withdrawn. 3) Amazingly, not only was a new site found, but word spread to the public of the fair's new location. 4) At the new site, fences that were supposed to facilitate ticket collection never materialized, and all attempts at gathering tickets were abandoned. 5) Crowd estimates of 30,000 kept rising; by the end of the three days, some estimated the crowd at 500,000. 6) Then, on opening night, it began to rain. 7) Off and on, throughout all three days, huge summer storms rolled over the gathering. 8) In spite of these problems, most people think of Woodstock not only as a fond memory but as the defining moment for an entire generation.

207. Which of the following would be the most appropriate title for this passage?
   a. Backstage at Woodstock
   b. Woodstock: From *The Band* to *The Who*
   c. Remembering Woodstock
   d. Woodstock: The Untold Story

208. Which of the following numbered sentences of the passage best represents an opinion rather than a fact?
   a. sentence 1
   b. sentence 2
   c. sentence 3
   d. sentence 4

209. Why is the word *amazingly* used in sentence 3?
   a. The time in which the site move was made and the word sent out was so short.
   b. The fair drew such an unexpectedly enormous crowd.
   c. There was such pressure by New York officials against holding the fair.
   d. The stormy weather was so unfavorable.

S E C T I O N

Nonfiction and Information Passages

I n this section, you will be dealing with nonfiction and information passages, such as the type you might find in a textbook. Mastering these types of passages and their questions is important, because they are increasingly being found in standardized tests. These passages are not necessarily more difficult than the ones you've already covered in the earlier chapters of this book. However, they do call more heavily for the special skill of making inferences, of identifying *implicit*, as opposed to *explicit*, ideas stated in the text.

Remember what you've learned so far. Look at structure. Look for the main idea of the passage. Consider the purpose for which the passage was written. What clues can you deduce from the writing style about the author's attitude toward the subject? Is the attitude positive? Negative? Objective? Try to pick out individual words that further each writer's intent and support each writer's opinion. If it helps, underline or make notes on important points. Active reading techniques like these will keep you focused on some very detailed reading comprehension passages.

The answers to this section begin on page 141.

Firefighters are often asked to speak to school and community groups about the importance of fire safety, particularly fire prevention and detection. Because smoke detectors reduce the risk of dying in a fire by half, firefighters often provide audiences with information on how to install these protective devices in their homes.

Specifically, they tell them these things: A smoke detector should be placed on each floor of a home. While sleeping, people are in particular danger of an emergent fire, and there must be a detector outside each sleeping area. A good site for a detector would be a hallway that runs between living spaces and bedrooms.

Because of the dead-air space that might be missed by turbulent hot air bouncing around above a fire, smoke detectors should be installed either on the ceiling at least four inches from the nearest wall, or high on a wall at least four, but no further than twelve, inches from the ceiling.

Detectors should not be mounted near windows, exterior doors, or other places where drafts might direct the smoke away from the unit. Nor should they be placed in kitchens and garages, where cooking and gas fumes are likely to cause false alarms.

210. Which organizational scheme does this list of instructions follow?
   a. hierarchical order
   b. comparison-contrast
   c. cause-and-effect
   d. chronological order by topic

211. What is the main focus of this passage?
   a. how firefighters carry out their responsibilities
   b. the proper installation of home smoke detectors
   c. the detection of dead-air space on walls and ceilings
   d. how smoke detectors prevent fires in homes

212. The passage implies that dead-air space is most likely to be found
   a. on a ceiling, between four and twelve inches from a wall.
   b. close to where a wall meets a ceiling.
   c. near an open window.
   d. in kitchens and garages.

213. The passage states that, compared with people who do not have smoke detectors, persons who live in homes with smoke detectors have a
   a. 50% better chance of surviving a fire.
   b. 50% better chance of preventing a fire.
   c. 75% better chance of detecting a hidden fire.
   d. 100% better chance of not being injured in a fire.

214. A smoke detector should NOT be installed near a window because
   a. outside fumes may trigger a false alarm.
   b. a draft may create dead-air space.
   c. a draft may pull smoke away from the detector.
   d. outside noises may muffle the sound of the detector.

215. The passage indicates that one responsibility of a firefighter is to
- **a.** install smoke detectors in the homes of residents in the community.
- **b.** check homes to see if smoke detectors have been properly installed.
- **c.** develop fire safety programs for community leaders and school teachers.
- **d.** speak to school children about the importance of preventing fires.

216. A smoke detector must always be placed
- **a.** outside at least one of the bedrooms on any level of the home.
- **b.** outside all bedrooms in a home.
- **c.** in all hallways of a home.
- **d.** in kitchens where fires are most likely to start.

Saving energy means saving money. Homeowners and renters know this basic fact, but they often don't know what kinds of adjustments they can make in their homes and apartments that will result in savings.

For those willing to spend some time and money to reap long-term energy savings, an energy audit is the way to go. An energy auditor will come into your home and assess its energy efficiency. The auditor will pinpoint areas of your home that use the most energy and offer solutions to lower your energy use and costs. Trained energy auditors know what to look for and can locate a variety of flaws that may be resulting in energy inefficiency, including inadequate insulation, construction flaws, and uneven heat distribution.

There are quicker and less costly measures that can be taken as well. One way to save money is to replace incandescent lights with fluorescents. This can result in a savings of more than 50% on your monthly lighting costs.

When it's time to replace old appliances, it's wise to spend a bit more for an energy-efficient model, and be sure that you are taking advantage of energy-saving settings already on your current refrigerator, dishwasher, washing machine, or dryer.

Windows provide another opportunity to cut your energy costs. Caulk old windows that might be leaky to prevent drafts, and choose double-paned windows if you're building an addition or replacing old windows.

Most areas of your home or apartment offer opportunities to save energy and money. The results are significant and are well worth the effort.

217. Which two main organizational schemes can be identified in this passage?
- **a.** hierarchical order and order by topic
- **b.** order by topic and cause and effect
- **c.** hierarchical order and chronological order
- **d.** chronological order and compare and contrast

218. Which of the following ideas is NOT included in this passage?
- **a.** You can reduce your $130 monthly lighting costs to $65 by using fluorescent bulbs instead of incandescent.
- **b.** Double-paned windows can cut energy costs.
- **c.** Your local energy company will send an energy auditor at your request.
- **d.** Some appliances have energy-saving settings.

219. Which of the following best expresses the main idea of this passage?
   a. There are many things a homeowner or renter can do to save energy and money.
   b. Hiring an energy auditor will save energy and money.
   c. Homeowners and renters don't know what they can do to save energy and money.
   d. Replacing windows and light bulbs are well worth the effort and cost.

220. According to the passage, which of the following would an energy auditor NOT do?
   a. Check for construction flaws.
   b. Look for problems with heat distribution.
   c. Offer solutions to lower your energy costs.
   d. Locate a variety of flaws that may result in energy inefficiency and fix them.

221. According the passage, double-paned windows
   a. are energy efficient.
   b. should only be used as replacement windows.
   c. should only be used in new additions to homes.
   d. will lower your heating costs by 50%.

Book clubs are a great way to meet new friends or keep in touch with old ones, while keeping up on your reading and participating in lively and intellectually stimulating discussions. If you're interested in starting a book club, you should consider the following options and recommendations.

   The first thing you'll need are members. Before recruiting, think carefully about how many people you want to participate and also what the club's focus will be. For example, some book clubs focus exclusively on fiction, others read nonfiction. Some are even more specific, focusing only on a particular genre such as mysteries, science fiction, or romance. Others have a more flexible and open focus. All of these possibilities can make for a great club, but it is important to decide on a focus at the outset so the guidelines will be clear to the group and prospective member.

   After setting the basic parameters, recruitment can begin. Notify friends and family, advertise in the local newspaper, and hang flyers on bulletin boards in local stores, colleges, libraries, and bookstores. When enough people express interest, schedule a kick-off meeting during which decisions will be made about specific guidelines that will ensure the club runs smoothly. This meeting will need to establish where the group will meet (rotating homes or a public venue such as a library or coffee shop); how often the group will meet, and on what day of the week and at what time; how long the meetings will be; how books will be chosen and by whom; who will lead the group (if anyone); and whether refreshments will be served and if so, who will supply them. By the end of this meeting, these guidelines should be set and a book selection and date for the first official meeting should be finalized.

   Planning and running a book club is not without challenges, but when a book club is run effectively, the experience can be extremely rewarding for everyone involved.

222. Which of the following organizational patterns is the main one used in the passage?
   a. chronological
   b. hierarchical
   c. comparison-contrast
   d. cause and effect

223. According to the passage, when starting a book club, the first thing a person should do is
   a. hang flyers in local establishments.
   b. put an ad in a local newspaper.
   c. decide on the focus and size of the club.
   d. decide when and where the group will meet.

224. Which of the following would NOT be covered during the book club's kick-off meeting?
   a. deciding on whether refreshments will be served.
   b. discussing and/or appointing a leader.
   c. choosing the club's first selection.
   d. identifying what kinds of books or genre will be the club's focus.

225. A good title for this passage would be
   a. Book Clubs: A Great Way to Make New Friends
   b. Starting a Successful Book Club: A Guide
   c. Five Easy Steps to Starting a Successful Book Club
   d. Reading in Groups: Sharing Knowledge, Nurturing Friendships

226. Which of the following is NOT something that successful book clubs should do?
   a. focus exclusively on one genre
   b. have guidelines about where and when to meet
   c. have a focus
   d. decide how to choose and who will choose book selections

227. Which of the following inferences can be drawn from the passage?
   a. Smaller groups are better for a variety of reasons.
   b. The social aspect of book clubs is more important than the intellectual.
   c. Starting your own book club is better than joining an existing one.
   d. When starting and running a book club, a casual approach is risky.

Last spring, employees of the Hartville Corporation organized a weeklong strike to protest poor working conditions and unreasonable company policies. The strike resulted in huge financial losses for the company and the threat of a national boycott on Hartville products. The situation resulted in the formation of an employee task force, supported by Hartville management, to review circumstances that led to the strike. The task-force findings follow:

- Hartville's overtime pay schedule is well below the national level, and overtime is mandatory at least once a week.

- Employees working in the manufacturing department have an alarmingly high rate of repetitive stress injury. The equipment they are working with is extremely old and dangerous and does not meet current health and safety standards. The task force recommended that equipment be evaluated and brought up-to-date immediately.

- Sick and personal day policies are unclear. Employees report conflicting and/or confusing policies relating to sick and personal days, which have resulted in numerous misunderstandings about procedures and allowances as well as unfair disciplinary action.

- In the past four years, five pregnant women with clean work records were terminated soon after their pregnancies were public. In all five cases, the grounds for firing were not specifically cited, although one of the employees was told by her immediate supervisor that new mothers make very unreliable employees.

- Hartville's upper management is largely unaware of the dissatisfaction of employees. There is evidence that middle management withholds vital information leading to upper management's underestimation of the severity of employee discontent.

228. Which of the following is the main organizational pattern used in the passage?
   a. chronological order
   b. hierarchical order
   c. order by topic
   d. cause and effect

229. According to the passage, why do Hartville employees have a high rate of repetitive stress injury?
   a. The equipment they use is broken.
   b. Their computer keyboards are outdated.
   c. Hartville's equipment is below standard.
   d. They are under a great deal of pressure at work.

230. According to the passage, which of the following was a specific task-force recommendation?
   a. Upper management at Hartville should be more involved in the day-to-day operation of the company.
   b. A new overtime pay policy should be implemented immediately.
   c. The pregnant women who were fired should file lawsuits.
   d. The equipment in the manufacturing department must be assessed.

231. According to the passage, one reason that the Hartville upper management is unresponsive is that

  a. they are more concerned with saving money than protecting employees.

  b. they are unaware of the degree of dissatisfaction among their employees.

  c. the company is about to be sold, and they are distracted.

  d. they have not been trained in the latest management techniques.

232. Which of the following is NOT in the passage?

  a. a finding about a problem within middle management

  b. a discussion of suspicious employee terminations

  c. a comparison between overtime pay at Hartville and the national average

  d. an outline of the policy relating to sick and personal days

Mental and physical health professionals may consider referring clients and patients to a music therapist for a number of reasons. It seems a particularly good choice for the social worker who is coordinating a client's case. Music therapists use music to establish a relationship with the patient and to improve the patient's health, using highly structured musical interactions. Patients and therapists may sing, play instruments, dance, compose, or simply listen to music.

The course of training for music therapists is comprehensive. In addition to formal musical and therapy training, music therapists are taught to discern what kinds of interventions will be most beneficial for each individual patient.

Because each patient is different and has different goals, the music therapist must be able to understand the patient's situation and choose the music and activities that will do the most toward helping the patient achieve his or her goals. The referring social worker can help this process by clearly communicating each client's history.

Although patients may develop their musical skills, that is not the main goal of music therapy. Any client who needs particular work on communication or on academic, emotional, and social skills, and who is not responding to traditional therapy, is an excellent candidate for music therapy.

233. Which of the following best organizes the main topics addressed in this passage?

  a. I.   The role of music therapy in social work
      II. Locating a music therapist
      III. Referring patients to music therapists

  b. I.   Using music in therapy
      II. A typical music-therapy intervention
      III. When to prescribe music therapy for sociopaths

  c. I.   Music therapy and social work
      II. Training for music therapists
      III. Skills addressed by music therapy

  d. I.   How to choose a music therapist
      II. When to refer to a music therapist
      III. Who benefits the most from music therapy

234. Which of the following would be the most appropriate title for this passage?
   a. How to Use Music to Combat Depression
   b. What Social Workers Need to Know about Music Therapy
   c. Training for a Career in Music Therapy
   d. The Social Worker as Music Therapist

235. According to information presented in the passage, music therapy can be prescribed for social work clients who
   a. need to develop coping skills.
   b. were orphaned as children.
   c. need to resolve family issues.
   d. need to improve social skills.

236. Which of the following inferences can be drawn from the passage?
   a. Music therapy can succeed where traditional therapies have failed.
   b. Music therapy is a relatively new field.
   c. Music therapy is particularly beneficial for young children.
   d. Music therapy is only appropriate in a limited number of circumstances.

In the summer, the Northern Hemisphere is slanted toward the sun, making the days longer and warmer than in winter. The first day of summer, June 21, is called summer solstice and is also the longest day of the year. However, June 21 marks the beginning of winter in the Southern Hemisphere, when that hemisphere is tilted away from the sun.

237. According to the passage, when it is summer in the Northern Hemisphere, it is _____ in the Southern Hemisphere.
   a. spring
   b. summer
   c. autumn
   d. winter

238. It can be inferred from the passage that, in the Southern Hemisphere, June 21 is the
   a. autumnal equinox.
   b. winter solstice.
   c. vernal equinox.
   d. summer solstice.

Jessie Street is sometimes called the Australian Eleanor Roosevelt. Like Roosevelt, Street lived a life of privilege, but she devoted her efforts to working for the rights of the disenfranchised, including workers, women, refugees, and Aborigines. In addition, she gained international fame when she was the only woman on the Australian delegation to the conference that founded the United Nations, just as Eleanor Roosevelt was for the United States.

239. Which of the following inferences may be drawn from the information presented in the passage?
   a. Eleanor Roosevelt and Jessie Street worked together to include women in the United Nations Charter.
   b. Usually, people who live lives of privilege do not spend much time participating in political activities.
   c. Discrimination in Australia is much worse than it ever was in the United States.
   d. At the time of the formation of the United Nations, few women were involved in international affairs.

Light pollution is a growing problem worldwide. Like other forms of pollution, light pollution degrades the quality of the environment. Where it was once possible to look up at the night sky and see thousands of twinkling stars in the inky blackness, one now sees little more than the yellow glare of urban sky-glow. When we lose the ability to connect visually with the vastness of the universe by looking up at the night sky, we lose our connection with something profoundly important to the human spirit, our sense of wonder.

240. The passage implies that the most serious damage done by light pollution is to our
   a. artistic appreciation.
   b. sense of physical well-being.
   c. cultural advancement.
   d. spiritual selves.

Moscow has a history of chaotic periods of war that ended with the destruction of a once largely wooden city and the building of a new city on top of the rubble of the old. The result is a layered city, with each tier holding information about a part of Russia's past. In some areas of the city, archaeologists have reached the layer from 1147, the year of Moscow's founding. Among the findings from the various periods of Moscow's history are carved bones, metal tools, pottery, glass, jewelry, and crosses.

241. From the passage, the reader can infer that
   a. the people of Moscow are more interested in modernization than in preservation.
   b. the Soviet government destroyed many of the historic buildings in Russia.
   c. Moscow is the oldest large city in Russia, founded in 1147.
   d. Moscow has a history of invasions, with each new conqueror razing past structures.

Authentic Dhurrie rugs are hand woven in India. Today, they are usually made of wool, but they are descendants of cotton floor and bed coverings. In fact, the name *Dhurrie* comes from the Indian word *dari*, which means *threads of cotton*. The rugs are noted for their soft colors, their varieties of design, and they make a stunning focal point for any living room or dining room.

242. Which of the following is the most likely intended audience for the passage?
   a. people studying traditional Indian culture
   b. people who are studying Indian domestic customs
   c. people learning to operate a rug loom
   d. people who enjoy interior decorating

Worldwide illiteracy rates have consistently declined in the last few decades. One of the major reasons for this decline is the sharp increase of literacy rates among young women, which is a result of specific campaigns designed to increase educational opportunities for girls. However, there are still an estimated 771 million illiterate adults in the world, about two-thirds of who are women.

243. Based on the passage, the author would tend to agree with which of the following statements?
   a. Men and women should have equal access to education.
   b. Males have a greater need for higher education than women.
   c. Worldwide, women need medical care more than the ability to read.
   d. It has been proven that women with increased education have fewer children.

Emperor Charlemagne of the Franks was crowned in 800 A.D. The Frankish Empire at that time extended over what is now Germany, Italy, and France. Charlemagne died in 814, but his brief reign marked the dawn of a distinctly European culture. The artists and thinkers that helped create this European civilization drew on the ancient texts of the Germanic, Celtic, Greek, Roman, Hebrew, and Christian worlds. _____ _____. Consequently, they were the groundwork for the laws, customs, and even attitudes of today's Europeans.

244. Which sentence, if inserted into the blank line in the passage, would be most consistent with the writer's purpose and intended audience?
   a. Cultural traditions function to identify members of a culture to one another and, also, to allow the individual to self-identify.
   b. Many of the traditions of these cultures remained active in Frankish society for centuries.
   c. When tradition is lacking or is not honored by the younger generation in a society, there is danger that the culture will be lost.
   d. It is unnecessary to discuss the origin of these traditions; it will only muddy the water.

245. Which of the following is the best meaning of the word *culture* as it is used in the passage?
   a. the fashionable class
   b. a community of interrelated individuals
   c. a partnership
   d. an organized group with a common goal

246. According to the passage, for how many years was Charlemagne Emperor of the Franks?
   a. 14 years
   b. 15 years
   c. 13 years
   d. 16 years

Coral reefs are among the most diverse and productive ecosystems on Earth. Consisting of both living and non-living components, this type of ecosystem is found in the warm, clear, shallow waters of tropical oceans worldwide. The functionality of the reefs ranges from providing food and shelter to fish and other forms of marine life to protecting the shore from the ill effects of erosion and underline{putrefaction}. In fact, reefs actually create land in tropical areas by formulating islands and contributing mass to continental shorelines.

Although coral looks like a plant, it is mainly comprised of the limestone skeleton of a tiny animal called a coral polyp. While corals are the main components of reef structure, they are not the only living participants. Coralline algae cement the myriad corals, and other miniature organisms such as tubeworms and mollusks contribute skeletons to this dense and diverse structure. Together, these living creatures construct many different types of tropical reefs.

247. Which of the following is the best meaning of the underlined word *putrefaction* as it is used in the first paragraph of the passage?
   a. purification
   b. decay
   c. jettison
   d. farming

248. Which of the following kinds of publications would most likely contain this passage?
   a. a history textbook
   b. an advanced marine biology textbook
   c. a collection of personal essays
   d. a general circulation magazine about science and nature

249. According to the passage, which of the following statements is NOT true?
   a. Coral reefs are beneficial for fish.
   b. Coral reefs are good for shorelines in tropical areas.
   c. Coral reefs are composed exclusively of coral.
   d. Coral reefs contain living and non-living components.

In 1899, Czar Nicholas II of Russia invited the nations of the world to a conference at The Hague. This conference—and a follow-up organized by Theodore Roosevelt in 1907—<u>ushered in</u> a period of vigorous growth in international law. This growth was in response to several factors, not the least of which was modern warfare's increasing potential for destruction. The recently concluded Civil War in the United States made this potential clear.

   During this growth, the subjects of international law were almost exclusively restricted to the relationships that countries had with one another. Issues of trade and warfare dominated both the disputes and the agreements of the period. _____, the developments of this period paved the way for further expansion of international law, which has occurred in the last several years. _____, organizations such as the United Nations and the International Court of Justice are greatly concerned not only with the way countries deal with one another, but with the ways in which they treat their own citizens.

250. Which words or phrases, if inserted in order into the blanks in the passage, would help the reader understand the sequence of the author's ideas?
   a. Therefore; In addition
   b. However; Now
   c. Furthermore; Yet
   d. Even if; On the other hand

251. According to the passage, what was the impact of the U.S. Civil War on the development of international law?
   a. It allowed armaments manufacturers to test new weapons.
   b. It diminished the influence of the United States internationally.
   c. It resulted in the suspension of agriculture exports from southern states.
   d. It highlighted the increasing destructive capabilities of modern warfare.

252. Which of the following is the best meaning of the underlined phrase *ushered in* as it is used in the passage?
   a. escorted
   b. progressed
   c. guarded
   d. heralded

A healthy diet with proper nutrition is essential for maintaining good overall health. Since the discovery of vitamins earlier in this century, people have routinely been taking vitamin supplements for this purpose. The Recommended Dietary Allowance (RDA) is a frequently used nutritional standard for maintaining optimal health. The RDA specifies the recommended amount of a number of nutrients for people in different age and sex groups. The National Research Council's Committee on Diet and Health has proposed a definition of the RDA to be that amount of a nutrient which meets the needs of 98% of the population.

The RDA approach _____ . First, it is based on the assumption that it is possible to accurately define nutritional requirements for a given group. However, individual nutritional requirements can vary widely within each group. The efficiency with which a person converts food intake into nutrients can also vary widely. Certain foods when eaten in combination actually prevent the absorption of nutrients. For example, spinach combined with milk reduces the amount of calcium available to the body from the milk. Also, the RDA approach specifies a different dietary requirement for each age and sex; however, it is clearly unrealistic to expect a homemaker to prepare a different menu for each family member. Still, although we cannot rely solely upon RDA to ensure our overall long-term health, it can be a useful guide so long as its limitations are recognized.

253. Which of the following would best fit in the blank in the first sentence of paragraph 2?
   a. is based on studies by respected nutritionists
   b. has a number of shortcomings
   c. has been debunked in the last few years
   d. is full of holes

254. With which of the following would the author most likely agree?
   a. The RDA approach should be replaced by a more realistic nutritional guide.
   b. The RDA approach should be supplemented with more specific nutritional guides.
   c. In spite of its flaws, the RDA approach is definitely the best guide to good nutrition.
   d. The RDA approach is most suitable for a large family.

Businesses today routinely keep track of large amounts of both financial and non-financial information. Sales departments keep track of current and potential customers; marketing departments keep track of product details and regional demographics; accounting departments keep track of financial data and issue reports. To be useful, all this data must be organized into a meaningful and useful system. Such a system is called a *management information system*, abbreviated MIS. The financial hub of the MIS is accounting.

Accounting is the information system that records, analyzes, and reports economic transactions, enabling decision makers to make informed choices when allocating scarce economic resources. It is a tool that enables the user, whether a business entity or an individual, to make wiser, more informed economic choices. It is an aid to planning, controlling, and evaluating a broad range of activities. A financial accounting system is intended for use by both the management of an organization and those outside the organization. Because it is important that financial accounting reports be interpreted correctly, financial accounting is subject to a set of _____ guidelines called "generally accepted accounting principles" (GAAP).

255. This passage is most likely taken from
  a. a newspaper column.
  b. a business textbook.
  c. an essay about modern business.
  d. a government document.

256. The word that would fit most correctly into the blank in the final sentence is
  a. discretionary.
  b. convenient.
  c. austere.
  d. stringent.

257. According to the information in the passage, which of the following is LEAST likely to be a function of accounting?
  a. helping business people make sound judgments
  b. assisting with the marketing of products
  c. producing reports of many different kinds of transactions
  d. assisting companies in important planning activities

Typically, people think of genius, whether it manifests in Mozart's composition of symphonies at age five or Einstein's discovery of relativity, as having a quality not just of the supernatural, but also of the eccentric. People see genius as a good abnormality; moreover, they think of genius as a completely unpredictable abnormality. Until recently, psychologists regarded the quirks of genius as too erratic to describe intelligibly; however, Anna Findley's ground-breaking study uncovers predictable patterns in the biographies of geniuses. These patterns do not dispel the common belief that there is a kind of supernatural intervention in the lives of unusually talented men and women, however, even though they occur with regularity. _____, Findley shows

that all geniuses experience three intensely productive periods in their lives, one of which always occurs shortly before their deaths; this is true whether the genius lives to 19 or 90.

258. Which word or phrase, if inserted into the blank space of the passage, best defines the relationship of the last sentence in the passage to the one preceding it?
  a. For example
  b. Despite this
  c. However
  d. In other words

259. According to the information presented in the passage, what is the general populace's opinion of genius?
  a. It is predictable and uncommon.
  b. It is supercilious and abnormal.
  c. It is unpredictable and erratic.
  d. It is extraordinary and erratic.

260. Which of the following would be the best title for this passage?
  a. Understanding Mozarts and Einsteins
  b. Predicting the Life of a Genius
  c. The Uncanny Patterns in the Lives of Geniuses
  d. Pattern and Disorder in the Lives of Geniuses

261. Given the information in the passage, which of the following statements is true?
  a. Anna Findley is a biographer.
  b. All geniuses are eccentric and unpredictable.
  c. Geniuses have three prolific times in their lives.
  d. Mozart discovered relativity.

O'Connell Street is the main thoroughfare of Dublin City. Although it is not a particularly long street, Dubliners will proudly tell the visitor that it is the widest street in all of Europe. This claim usually meets with protests, especially from French tourists, claiming the Champs Elysees of Paris as Europe's widest street. But the witty Dubliner will not easily relinquish bragging rights and will <u>trump</u> the French visitor with a fine distinction: The Champs Elysees is a *boulevard*; O'Connell is a *street*.

Divided by several important monuments running the length of its center, the street is named for Daniel O'Connell, an Irish patriot. _____. O'Connell stands high above the unhurried crowds of shoppers, business people, and students on a sturdy column, surrounded by four serene angels seated at each corner of the monument's base. Further up the street is the famous General Post Office that locals affectionately call the GPO. During the 1916 rebellion, the GPO was taken over from British rule and occupied by Irish rebels, sparking weeks of armed combat in the city's center. To this day, the angels of O'Connell's monument bear the marks of the fighting: One sits reading calmly, apparently unaware of the bullet hole dimpling her upper arm; another, reaching out to stroke the ears of a huge bronze Irish wolfhound has survived what should be a mortal wound to her heart.

262. Which sentence, if inserted in the blank space in the passage, would be the most correct and contribute the most pertinent information to that paragraph?
  a. His monument stands at the lower end of the road, that is, the end closest to the river Liffey that bisects Dublin.
  b. Other monuments along the street include statues to Charles Parnell, Anna Livia Plurabelle, and James Joyce.
  c. Dublin tourist buses leave from this site every 20 minutes.
  d. Daniel O'Connell was an important Irish nationalist, who died before the 1916 rebellion.

263. Which of the following would be the best title for this passage?
  a. Dublin's Famous Monuments
  b. The Irish Take Pride in Their Capital City
  c. The Widest Street in Europe
  d. Sights and History on Dublin's O'Connell Street

264. What is the best definition for the underlined word *trump* as it is used in the first paragraph of the passage?
  a. to trumpet loudly, to blare or drown out
  b. to trample
  c. to get the better of by using a key or hidden resource
  d. to devise a fraud, to employ trickery

265. With which of the following statements about the people of Dublin would the author of the passage most likely agree?
  a. They are proud of their history but lack industry.
  b. They are playful and tricky.
  c. They are rebellious and do not like tourists.
  d. They are witty and relaxed.

The subject of the next two passages is the same, but the way they are written is different. Read them carefully and answer the questions.

Excerpt from Chamber of Commerce brochure

Dilly's Deli provides a dining experience like no other! A rustic atmosphere, along with delicious food, provide an opportunity to soak up the local flavor. Recently relocated to the old market area, Dilly's is especially popular for lunch. At the counter, you can place your order for one of Dilly's three daily lunch specials or one of several sandwiches, all at reasonable prices. Once you get your food, choose a seat at one of the four charming communal tables. By the time you are ready to carry your paper plate to the trash bin, you have experienced some of the best food and one of the most charming companies our city has to offer.

Restaurant review

Yesterday, I was exposed to what has been called "a dining experience like no other." At lunchtime, Dilly's Deli is so crowded, I wondered when the fire marshal had last visited the establishment. The line snaked out the door to the corner, and by the time I reached the counter, I was freezing. I decided on the hamburger steak special; the other specials being liver and onions or tuna casserole. Each special is offered with two side dishes, but there was no potato salad left and the green beans were cooked nearly beyond recognition. I chose the gelatin of the day and what turned out to be the blandest coleslaw I have ever eaten.

At Dilly's, you sit at one of four long tables. The couple sitting across from me was having an argument. The truck driver next to me told me more than I wanted to know about highway taxes. After I had tasted all of the food on my plate, I rose to leave, whereupon one of the people working behind the counter yelled at me to clean up after myself. Throwing away that plate of food was the most enjoyable part of dining at Dilly's.

266. If you go to lunch at Dilly's Deli, you could expect to see
   a. a long line of customers.
   b. the fire marshal.
   c. the restaurant critic from the newspaper.
   d. homemade pie.

267. Both passages suggest that if you eat lunch at Dilly's Deli, you should expect to
   a. sit next to a truck driver.
   b. place your order with the waiter who comes to your table.
   c. dress warmly.
   d. carry your own food to your table.

268. Which of the following illustrates the restaurant critic's opinion of the food at Dilly's Deli?
   a. "At Dilly's, you sit at one of four long tables."
   b. "At lunchtime, Dilly's Deli is so crowded, I wondered when the fire marshal had last visited the establishment."
   c. "After I had tasted all of the food on my plate, I rose to leave, whereupon one of the people working behind the counter yelled at me to clean up after myself."
   d. "Throwing away that plate of food was the most enjoyable part of dining at Dilly's."

269. The main purpose of the restaurant review is to
   a. tell people they probably don't want to eat at Dilly's Deli.
   b. make fun of couples who argue in public.
   c. recommend the hamburger steak special.
   d. warn people that Dilly's Deli tends to be crowded.

270. The main purpose of the Chamber of Commerce brochure is to
   a. profile the owner of Dilly's Deli.
   b. describe in detail the food served at Dilly's Deli.
   c. encourage people to eat at Dilly's Deli.
   d. explain the historical significance of the Dilly's Deli Building.

Cuttlefish are intriguing little animals. The cuttlefish resembles a rather large squid and is, like the octopus, a member of the order of cephalopods. Although they are not considered the most highly evolved of the cephalopods, they are extremely intelligent. While observing them, it is hard to tell who is doing the observing, you or the cuttlefish, especially since the eye of the cuttlefish is similar in structure to the human eye. Cuttlefish are also highly mobile and fast creatures. They come equipped with a small jet located just below the tentacles that can expel water to help them move. Ribbons of flexible fins on each side of the body allow cuttlefish to hover, move, stop, and start. _____.

The cuttlefish is sometimes referred to as the "chameleon of the sea" because it can change its skin color and pattern instantaneously. Masters of camouflage, they can blend into any environment for protection, but they are also capable of the most imaginative displays of iridescent, brilliant color and intricate designs, which scientists believe they use for communication and for mating displays. However, judging from the riot of ornaments and hues cuttlefish produce, it is hard not to believe they paint themselves so beautifully just for the sheer joy of it. At the very least, cuttlefish conversation must be the most sparkling in all the sea.

271. Which of the following sentences, if inserted into the blank line, would best sum up the first paragraph and lead into the next.
   a. The cuttlefish can be cooked and eaten like its less tender relatives, the squid and octopus, but must still be tenderized before cooking in order not to be exceedingly chewy.
   b. On a scuba dive when you're observing cuttlefish, it is best to move slowly because cuttlefish have excellent eyesight and will probably see you first.
   c. Cuttlefish do not have an exoskeleton; instead, their skin is covered with chromataphors.
   d. By far, their most intriguing characteristic is their ability to change their body color and pattern.

272. Which of the following is correct according to the information given in the passage?

a. Cuttlefish are a type of squid.

b. Cuttlefish use jet propulsion as one form of locomotion.

c. The cuttlefish does not have an exoskeleton.

d. Cuttlefish are the most intelligent cephalopods.

273. Which of the following best outlines the main topics addressed in the passage?

a. I. Explanation of why cuttlefish are intriguing

II. Communication skills of cuttlefish

b. I. Classification and difficulties of observing cuttlefish

II. Scientific explanation of modes of cuttlefish communication

c. I. Explanation of the cuttlefish's method of locomotion

II. Description of color displays in mating behavior

d. I. General classification and characteristics of cuttlefish

II. Uses and beauty of the cuttlefish's ability to change color

274. Which of the following best describes the purpose of the author in the passage?

a. to prove the intelligence of cuttlefish

b. to explain the communication habits of cuttlefish

c. to produce a fanciful description of the "chameleon of the sea"

d. to describe the "chameleon of the sea" informatively and entertainingly

During those barren winter months, with windows overlooking long-dead gardens, leafless trees, and lawns that seem to have an ashy look about them, nothing soothes the jangled nerves more than the vibrant green of plants surrounding the living spaces of one's home. People browse through garden stores just to get a whiff of chlorophyll and to choose a plant or two to bring spring back into their winter-gray lives.

Now there is even more of a need for "the green," in light of recent articles warning us of the hazards of chemicals that we, ourselves, introduce into our homes. Each time we bring clothes home from the cleaners, we release those chemicals into the closed-in air of our dwellings. Every cleanser releases its own assortment of fumes. Some of the chemicals are formaldehyde, chlorine, benzene, styrene, etc. Read the labels on many home products, the ingredients aren't even listed! During the winter, when those same windows are shut tight, we breathe in these chemicals—causing symptoms much like allergies. In fact, most people probably dismiss the effects of these chemicals simply as a flare up of some allergy or other. The truth is that we are experiencing a syndrome that is called Multiple Chemical Sensitivity. Now, what has this got to do with green plants? Everything healthy! Research has been conducted with two types of plants that have actually removed much of these harmful chemicals from the air.

The two plants that seem to be the best bet for ridding one's home of such chemicals are ferns and palms. These plants release moisture as part of photosynthesis and, as they do, pull chemicals from the air into their leaves. Even NASA has conducted some greenhouse experiments for long-term space exploration. Within hours, their plants [palms] had removed almost all traces of formaldehyde in the room. Both species of plants are ancient, dating back more than a hundred million years. Another trait they share is that they both live long lives, 100 years or more. This we expect from trees, but ferns and palms are plants; plants that can grow to 65 feet in the proper setting! Even their individual leaves live for one to two years [ferns] and one to nine years [palms]. Perhaps it is their primal qualities that have contributed to their ability to purify their environment.

275. What is the main idea of the passage?
   a. Our homes are full of contaminants.
   b. Our allergies are caused by chemicals found in the home.
   c. All plants release moisture in the home.
   d. Certain plants can purify the home of many harmful chemicals.

276. According to the passage, when a few harmful chemicals combine, they can
   a. cause us to experience allergies.
   b. cause a monumental task for homeowners.
   c. contribute to a syndrome called Multiple Chemical Sensitivity.
   d. contribute to photosynthesis in plants.

277. The passage indicates that research
   a. has only been conducted using specific plants.
   b. has only been conducted by NASA.
   c. has not identified the sources of these chemical impurities.
   d. has only benefited long term space exploration.

278. The passage infers a relationship between the antiquity of ferns and palms and their ability to
- **a.** live long.
- **b.** purify the air.
- **c.** grow leaves that live long.
- **d.** react successfully in research experiments.

279. A good title for this passage is
- **a.** Research in the New Millennium.
- **b.** Home Dangers.
- **c.** Common Houseplants May Purify Your Home.
- **d.** NASA Experiment Finds the Cure.

Despite their similarities, the pyramids of Egypt and Mesoamerica seem to be unrelated because of distinct differences in the time of construction as well as their design and function. Historians have discovered that the construction of the pyramids in Egypt and Mesoamerica are separated by over 2,000 years. The Egyptians used only cut stone quarried many miles away from the pyramid sites—a construction method that enabled them to construct sturdy buildings that could withstand the test of time.

On the other hand, the pyramids of Mesoamerica were not built to withstand the ravages of time. Rather, the step pyramids rose in tiers, on the top of which a small temple was erected. Unlike the Egyptians, they used irregular stones.

Also, they did not share the same basic design function. While the Egyptian pyramids were private tombs meant to seperate the pharaoh's remains from the mainstream of society and protect him for <u>eternity</u>, the pyramids of Mesoamerica were primarily public temples of ritual and celebration.

280. The main idea of this passage is best summed up in which statement?
- **a.** Pyramids in Egypt and Mesoamerica are similar.
- **b.** Egyptians assisted Mesoamerican pyramid builders.
- **c.** Pyramids in Egypt and Mesoamerica have distinct differences.
- **d.** Scientists do not know who built the pyramids.

281. This passage best supports the statement that
- **a.** the Egyptians used stone quarried many miles away from the pyramid site.
- **b.** the pyramids of Mesoamerica were built to last for eternity.
- **c.** the Egyptian pyramids were public tombs.
- **d.** the Egyptian and Mesoamerican pyramids were built during the same time period.

282. The passage best supports the statement that
- **a.** Egyptian and Mesoamerican pyramids shared the same design function.
- **b.** both pyramids were used as temples of ritual and celebration.
- **c.** Egyptian and Mesoamerican pyramids shared the same construction methods.
- **d.** Mesoamerican pyramids were used for ritual and celebration.

283. The underlined word *eternity* in the passage most nearly means which of the following?
- **a.** for a short time
- **b.** temporary
- **c.** for all time
- **d.** never

Born in Joplin, Missouri, in 1902, Langston Hughes grew up to become a prominent writer of the black American experience. During his high school years in Illinois, he began writing poetry. In November 1924, he moved to Harlem, New York, where his life and work contributed greatly to the Harlem Renaissance of the 1920s. In his writing, Langston Hughes portrayed black life in America from the 1920s through the 1960s. He wrote novels, short stories, and plays, as well as poetry. Also, he is known for his engagement with the world of jazz and the influence it had on his writing, as in "Montage of a Dream Deferred." Hughes did not personalize his stories because he wanted readers to draw their own conclusions about the experiences of blacks in America.

284. Why didn't Hughes personalize his stories?
  a. He did not have enough personal experiences.
  b. He only wanted to write about the Harlem jazz experience.
  c. He wanted readers to draw their own conclusions about the black experience.
  d. He wanted to keep his personal life a secret.

285. In his poem, "Montage of a Dream Deferred," what influenced his writing?
  a. Renaissance music
  b. his travel experience
  c. his high school years
  d. the world of jazz

286. Langston Hughes was known for which of the following?
  a. writing poems and plays only
  b. writing novels and short stories only
  c. writing plays and short stories only
  d. writing novels, short stories, plays, and poems

287. His life and work contributed greatly to which of the following?
  a. the Harlem Renaissance
  b. the jazz world
  c. Joplin, Missouri
  d. his high school in Illinois

Reading Charts and Graphs, Understanding Directions

This is a section with questions that can be applied to situations you find in everyday life. On the job, in your school, at the train station, in the grocery store, or in many other ordinary situations, you might find yourself trying to access information from a graph, chart, or table. You may even find situations where you have to listen to and act upon written or verbal directions.

Unlike other sections in this book, the questions you answer in this section are based on concrete information, rather than hidden or implied material within the text. So, the most important thing is to pay attention to every detail. Read every set of directions as many times as necessary. Also, read the title and footnotes carefully.

The ability to completely understand directions, graphs, charts, and tables is vital in today's Information Age, but as you may know, it is not always easy. With a little practice, these types of questions can be the easiest. This section gives you ample opportunity to hone your skills.

The answers to this section begin on page 146.

Below and on the following pages are tables that are typical of the type you might be asked to read in a text-book or on the job. Note their simplicity and economy.

THE FUJITA-PEARSON TORNADO INTENSITY SCALE		
CLASSIFICATION	WIND SPEED	DAMAGE
F0	40–72 mph	Mild
F1	73–112 mph	Moderate
F2	113–157 mph	Significant
F3	158–206 mph	Severe
F4	207–260 mph	Devastating
F5	260–319 mph	Incredible
F6	319–379 mph	Inconceivable

288. A tornado with a wind speed of 143 mph would be assigned which classification?
   a. F0
   b. F1
   c. F2
   d. F3

289. The names of the categories in the third column, labeled "Damage," could best be described as
   a. scientific.
   b. descriptive.
   c. objective.
   d. whimsical.

	FOREST FIRES, TRI-COUNTY AREA JUNE 2005		
DATE	AREA	NUMBER OF ACRES BURNED	PROBABLE CAUSE
June 2	Burgaw Grove	115	Lightning
June 3	Fenner Forest	200	Campfire
June 7	Voorhees Air Base Training Site	400	Equipment Use
June 12	Murphy County Nature Reserve	495	Children
June 13	Knoblock Mountain	200	Miscellaneous
June 14	Cougar Run Ski Center	160	Unknown
June 17	Fenner Forest	120	Campfire
June 19	Stone River State Park	526	Arson
June 21	Burgaw Grove	499	Smoking
June 25	Bramley Acres Resort	1,200	Arson
June 28	Hanesboro Crossing	320	Lightning
June 30	Stone River State Park	167	Campfire

290. One week before the Cougar Run Ski Center fire, where did a fire occur?
   a. Fenner Forest
   b. Voorhees Air Base Training Site
   c. Murphy County Nature Reserve
   d. Burgaw Grove

291. According to the table, lightning fires
   a. occurred at Burgaw Grove and Fenner Forest.
   b. consumed less than 500 acres.
   c. consumed more acres than suspected arson fires.
   d. occurred more frequently than fires caused by campfires.

292. Which of the following incidents at Hanesboro Crossing would be considered an act of nature?
   a. A group of rowdy teenagers tossed a match into a tent.
   b. A deer hunter lighting a cigarette accidentally tossed a match too close to a dry shrub.
   c. An inexperienced camper filled a camp stove with gasoline and it exploded.
   d. Lightning struck a tree in the forest.

HURST COUNTY TOWNS, NUMBER OF DAYS WITHOUT SIGNIFICANT PRECIPITATION*		
TOWN	**NUMBER OF DAYS**	**STATUS****
Riderville	38	level two
Adams	25	level one
Parkston	74	level three
Kings Hill	28	level two
West Granville	50	level three
Braxton	23	level three
Chase Crossing	53	level four
Livingston Center	45	level three

* *Less than half an inch in a 48-hour period.*
** *The higher the level, the greater potential for fire.*

293. The status of the town with the most number of days without significant precipitation is
a. level one.
b. level two.
c. level three.
d. level four.

294. Compared to Kings Hill, Chase Crossing
a. is more likely to experience a fire.
b. is less likely to experience a fire.
c. is just as likely to experience a fire.
d. has gone a shorter period of time without significant precipitation.

DISTRIBUTION OF OCCUPATIONS OF 200 ADULT MALES IN THE BAIDYA CASTE, MADARIPUR VILLAGE, BENGAL, 1914	
OCCUPATION	**NUMBER**
farmers	02
government service, clerks	44
lawyers	06
newspapers and presses	05
no occupation	25
not recorded	08
students	68
teachers	11
trade and commerce	23
other	08

295. The *largest* number of men in the Baidya caste of Madaripur are involved in which field?
a. education
b. agriculture
c. government
d. publishing

296. The *smallest* number of men in the Baidya caste of Madaripur are involved in which field?
a. education
b. agriculture
c. government
d. publishing

| MEN'S AND WOMEN'S TABLE TENNIS, SUMMER OLYMPICS 2004 | | | | |
COUNTRY	GOLD	SILVER	BRONZE	TOTAL
China	3	1	2	6
Korea	1	1	1	3
Denmark	0	0	1	1

| WOMEN'S TABLE TENNIS, SUMMER OLYMPICS 2004 | | | | |
COUNTRY	GOLD	SILVER	BRONZE	TOTAL
China	2	0	1	3
Korea	0	1	1	2
Hong Kong	0	0	0	0

| MEN'S TABLE TENNIS, SUMMER OLYMPICS 2004 | | | | |
COUNTRY	GOLD	SILVER	BRONZE	TOTAL
China	1	1	1	3
Demark	0	0	1	1
Hong Kong	0	1	0	1

297. According to the Men's and Women's Table Tennis chart, which country received the most medals for both men and women in table tennis?
a. China
b. Korea
c. Denmark
d. Hong Kong

298. In the Men's Table Tennis competition, which country only won a bronze medal?
a. China
b. Hong Kong
c. Denmark
d. Korea

299. In which competition did Korea win an equal number of gold, silver, and bronze medals?
a. the Men's competition
b. the Women's competition
c. no equal amounts
d. the combined Men's and Women's competition

300. Which of the following countries won one bronze medal and no other medals?
a. Korea
b. Denmark
c. China
d. Hong Kong

| | MOUNT WASHINGTON, NEW HAMPSHIRE WEATHER DATA ELEVATION: 6,288 FEET   LATITUDE: 44 16N   LONGITUDE: 071 18W | | | |
YEARLY	JANUARY	FEBRUARY	MARCH	APRIL
Average Temperature				
27° (Fahrenheit)	6°	6°	13°	23°
Average Precipitation				
90.7 inches	7.1 inches	7.4 inches	7.9 inches	7.2 inches
Average Snowfall				
41 inches	40 inches	40.8 inches	42.5 inches	31.3 inches

301. What is the average snowfall for the month of February?
  a. 7.4 inches
  b. 13 inches
  c. 40 inches
  d. 40.8 inches

302. What is the average temperature for the month of April?
  a. 6°
  b. 13°
  c. 23°
  d. 31.3°

303. What is the average snowfall for the year?
  a. 41 inches
  b. 40 inches
  c. 42.5 inches
  d. 31.3 inches

304. What is the average precipitation for the month of March?
  a. 90.7 inches
  b. 7.4 inches
  c. 7.9 inches
  d. 7.2 inches

Body Mass Index (BMI) relates a person's weight to his or her height. Clinical researchers use the following guide-lines regarding a person's BMI and possible health risks.

BMI CATEGORY	HEALTH RISK BASED SOLELY ON BMI	RISK ADJUSTED FOR THE PRESENCE OF OTHER HEALTH CONDITIONS AND/OR RISK FACTORS
19–24	Minimal	Low
25–26	Low	Moderate
27–29	Moderate	High
30–34	High	Very high
35–39	Very high	Extremely high

305. In the 35–39 BMI range, what is the risk based solely on BMI?
   a. low
   b. moderate
   c. high
   d. very high

306. What range BMI is considered a minimal health risk?
   a. 19–24
   b. 25–26
   c. 27–29
   d. 30–34

307. All these are categories for the BMI chart except which one?
   a. BMI
   b. Health Risk l
   c. Risk Adjusted for Other Health Conditions
   d. heart rate

308. In the 27–29 BMI range, what is the risk based solely on BMI?
   a. minimal
   b. low
   c. moderate
   d. high

For many occupations, workers are asked to read policy, work instructions, and rules. Following are a number of job-related passages. Start with these relatively simple notices posted for workers.

Notice 1

All drivers are responsible for refueling their vehicles at the end of each shift. All other routine maintenance should be performed by maintenance-department personnel, who are also responsible for maintaining service records. If a driver believes a vehicle is in need of mechanical repair, the driver should fill out the pink repair requisition form and give it to the shift supervisor. The driver should also notify the shift supervisor verbally whether, in the driver's opinion, the vehicle must be repaired immediately or may be driven until the end of the shift.

309. If a vehicle is due to have the oil changed, whose responsibility is it?
   a. maintenance-department personnel
   b. the drivers at the end of their shifts
   c. shift supervisors
   d. outside service mechanics

310. The passage implies that the vehicles
   a. are refueled when they have less than half a tank of gas.
   b. have the oil changed every 1,000 miles.
   c. are refueled at the end of every shift.
   d. are in frequent need of repair.

Notice 2

Beginning next month, the city will institute a program intended to remove graffiti from city-owned delivery trucks. Any truck that finishes its assigned route before the end of the driver's shift will return to its lot where supervisors will provide materials for that driver to use while cleaning the truck. Because the length of time it takes to complete different tasks and routes vary, trucks within the same department will no longer be assigned to specific routes but will be rotated among the routes. Therefore, drivers should no longer leave personal items in the trucks, because they will not necessarily be driving the same truck each day, as they did in the past.

311. According to the passage, the removal of graffiti from trucks will be done by
   a. a small group of drivers specifically assigned to the task.
   b. custodians who work for the city.
   c. any supervisor or driver who finishes a route first.
   d. each driver as that driver finishes the assigned route.

312. According to the passage, routes within particular departments
   a. vary in the amount of time they take to complete.
   b. vary in the amount of graffiti they are likely to have on them.
   c. are all approximately of equal length.
   d. vary according to the truck's driver.

313. According to the passage, prior to instituting the graffiti clean-up program, city workers
   a. were not responsible for cleaning the trucks.
   b. had to repaint the trucks at intervals.
   c. usually drove the same truck each workday.
   d. were not allowed to leave personal belongings in the trucks.

Memo to Supervisory Personnel

Members of your investigative team may have skills and abilities of which you are not aware. As investigator in charge of a case, you should seek out and take advantage of potential talent in all the members of your team. Whenever a new case is given to your team, it is usually a good idea to have all the members devise ideas and suggestions about all aspects of the case, rather than insisting that each member stick rigidly to his or her narrow area of expertise. This way, you are likely to discover special investigative skills you never suspected your team members had. It's worthwhile to take extra time to explore all your team's talents.

314. The paragraph best supports the statement that a single member of an investigative team
- **a.** may have abilities that the leader of the team doesn't know.
- **b.** usually stands out as having more ideas than other members do.
- **c.** should be assigned the task of discovering the whole team's talents.
- **d.** can have more skills and abilities than all the rest.

All Drivers Take Note

The City Transit supervisors have received numerous complaints over the last several weeks about buses on several routes <u>running hot</u>. Drivers are reminded that each route has several checkpoints at which drivers should check the time. If the bus is ahead of schedule, drivers should delay at the checkpoint until it is the proper time to leave. If traffic makes it unsafe for a driver to delay at a particular checkpoint, the driver should proceed at a reasonable speed to the next stop and hold there until the bus is back on schedule.

315. According to the passage, when a bus is *running hot*, it means
- **a.** the bus is going too fast and the engine is overheating.
- **b.** the bus is running ahead of schedule.
- **c.** the bus is running behind schedule.
- **d.** passengers are complaining about the bus being off schedule.

316. The main point of the passage is that drivers should
- **a.** stop their buses when traffic is unsafe.
- **b.** drive at a reasonable speed.
- **c.** check the time at every stop.
- **d.** see that their buses run on schedule.

Important Warning

Only certain people are qualified to handle hazardous waste. Hazardous waste is defined as any waste designated by the U.S. Environmental Protection Agency as hazardous. If you are unclear whether a particular item is hazardous, you should not handle the item but should instead notify a supervisor of the Sanitation Department.

317. Hazardous waste is defined as
    a. anything too dangerous to handle.
    b. waste picked up by special sanitation trucks.
    c. anything so designated by the U.S. Environmental Protection Agency.
    d. waste not allowed to be placed alongside regular residential garbage.

318. Sanitation Worker Harris comes upon a container of cleaning solvent along with the regular garbage in front of a residence. The container does not list the contents of the cleaner. Therefore, according to the directions, Harris should
    a. assume the solvent is safe and deposit it in the sanitation truck.
    b. leave a note for the residents, asking them to list the contents of the solvent.
    c. simply leave the container on the curb.
    d. contact the supervisor for directions.

Notice of Mandatory Refresher Training Course

During the next ten months, all bus operators with two or more years of service will be required to have completed 20 hours of refresher training on one of the Vehicle Maneuvering Training Buses.

Instructors who have used this new technology report that trainees develop skills more quickly than with traditional training methods. In refresher training, this new system reinforces defensive driving skills and safe driving habits. Drivers can also check their reaction times and hand-eye coordination.

As an added benefit, the city expects to save money with the simulators, because the new system reduces the amount of training time in an actual bus—saving on parts, fuel, and other operating expenses.

319. All bus operators are required to do which of the following?
    a. Receive training in defensive driving and operating a computer.
    b. Complete ten months of refresher driver training.
    c. Train new drivers on how to operate a simulator.
    d. Complete 20 hours of training on a simulator.

320. The main purpose of the refresher training course on the simulator is to
    a. make sure that all bus operators are maintaining proper driving habits.
    b. give experienced bus operators an opportunity to learn new driving techniques.
    c. help all bus operators to develop hand-eye coordination.
    d. reduce the city's operating budget.

Notice: Training to Begin for F.A.S.T. Membership

A training calendar and schedule for Fire Agency Specialties Team (F.A.S.T.) membership is available in this office to all applicants for F.A.S.T. membership. Training will take place the third week of each month. Classes will be taught on Monday afternoons, Wednesday evenings, and Saturday afternoons.

So that the F.A.S.T. can maintain a high level of efficiency and preparedness for emergency response situations, its members must meet certain requirements.

First, in order for you to be considered for membership on F.A.S.T., your department must be a member of the F.A.S.T. organization, and you must have written permission from your fire chief or your department's highest ranking administrator.

Once active, you must meet further requirements to maintain active status. These include completion of technician-level training and certification in hazardous material (hazmat) operations. In addition, after becoming a member, you must also attend a minimum of 50% of all drills conducted by F.A.S.T. and go to at least one F.A.S.T. conference. You may qualify for alternative credit for drills by proving previous experience in actual hazmat emergency response.

If you fail to meet minimum requirements, you will be considered inactive, and the director of your team will be notified. You will be placed back on active status only after you complete the training necessary to meet the minimum requirements.

321. Potential F.A.S.T. members can attend less than half of F.A.S.T. drills if they
  a. complete technician-level training requirements.
  b. indicate prior real emergency experience.
  c. receive permission from their fire chief.
  d. enroll in three weekly training sessions.

322. Which of the following is the main subject of the passage?
  a. preparing for hazmat certification
  b. the main goal of F.A.S.T.
  c. completing F.A.S.T. membership requirements
  d. learning about your department's F.A.S.T. membership

323. Applicants must be available for training
  a. three days each month.
  b. three days each week.
  c. every third month.
  d. for 50% of classes.

One of the most common injuries teenagers and adults experience is a sprained ankle. A sprain occurs when the ligaments of a joint are twisted and possibly torn. Ligaments are bands of stringy fibers that hold the bones of a joint in position. A sprain can occur from a sudden wrenching at the joint, or a stretching or tearing of the fibers of the ligaments. The injured area usually swells and becomes black and blue. Stepping off the sidewalk at the wrong angle or having one foot land in a hole while jogging can leave you rolling on the ground in agony with an ankle on fire! If you cannot walk without experiencing intense pain, you must seek medical help. If the pain is manageable, and you can walk, here are three words to help you remember how to treat yourself:

- Elevate
- Cool
- Bandage

As soon as there is injury to that ligament, there will be a certain amount of bleeding under the skin. Once the blood pools around the damaged blood vessels, inflammation and swelling occur. The pressure from the swelling results in additional stress and tenderness to the region. In order to minimize the degree of swelling, lie down as soon as possible and keep the ankle elevated so that it is actually higher than your heart. Next, to shrink the blood vessels and keep bleeding (hence bruising) to a minimum, apply a cold pack. After 20 minutes, take the pack off, wait half an hour, and then reapply. This can be done several times a day for a total of three days.

Never leave a cold pack on for more than 20 minutes at a time. Reducing the temperature in that area for an extended period of time signals the body to *increase* blood flow to raise the body temperature! Therefore, one inadvertently triggers more blood distribution to the affected area by leaving a cold pack on for too long! Finally, bandage the ankle. Be careful not to wind it too tightly; doing so can restrict blood flow and cause harm to the entire foot.

324. The main idea of the passage is to
   a. describe sprains to the ligaments.
   b. explain how to bandage injuries.
   c. explain how to treat your own sprained ankle.
   d. explain how the temperature of a wound is important.

325. According to the passage, a sprain is caused by
   a. enlarged blood vessels in the foot.
   b. fluctuating temperature signaling the elevation of body temperature.
   c. torn tissue in the ball of the foot.
   d. torn or twisted ligament fibers that hold the joint in position.

326. Which of the following is NOT mentioned as a warning?

a. If there is intense pain, seek medical attention.

b. Do not wind the bandage too tightly.

c. Do not put your ankle near the fire.

d. Do not keep the cold pack on for more than 20 minutes at a time.

327. According to the directions, once the initial cold pack is removed, what is to be done?

a. Begin wrapping the bandage.

b. Begin wrapping by encircling the ball of the foot twice.

c. Wait 20 minutes and then reapply the ice pack for 30 minutes.

d. Wait 30 minutes and then reapply the ice pack for 20 minutes.

328. It can be inferred that the black-and-blue symptom of the sprain is due to

a. torn fibers of ligaments.

b. too tight of a bandage.

c. bleeding under the skin.

d. dirt ground into the wound from the fall.

SECTION

8 ▶ Analyzing and Interpreting Poems

Poetry scares some people, mainly because they believe that poems have hidden meanings. A good way to approach poetry is by reading closely for the literal meaning. In reality, poetry compresses the language into small sentences or phrases, so it just seems that the meanings are hidden. Ask yourself, what is that poet's view on the subject? If you add a few of your own thoughts and experiences, you can uncover what has been left out. Think of it as frozen orange juice. Add water and you have the entire amount. Also, remember that poets compare objects to other objects . . . just like the frozen orange-juice metaphor. Think back to Section 2, Analogies, and remember the way you made comparisons there.

As you begin to read the poems in this section, it is important to understand who is speaking in the poem. (The speaker may not be the poet.) Once you can identify the narrator, you should be able to get an idea of the narrator's attitude toward the subject, and this is easily discovered by the author's word choice. Through the images that the words make, you should be able to answer the questions correctly.

The answers to this section begin page 147.

The following poem is by Alfred, Lord Tennyson. Consider the title of this poem as a guide to meaning.

The Eagle

He clasps the crag with crooked hands;
Close to the sun in lonely lands,
Ringed with the <u>azure world</u> he stands.

The wrinkled sea beneath him crawls;
He watches from his mountain walls,
And like a thunderbolt he falls.

329. Given the tone of the poem, and noting especially the last line, what is the eagle most likely doing in the poem?
   a. dying of old age
   b. hunting prey
   c. learning joyfully to fly
   d. keeping watch over a nest of young eagles

330. To which of the following do the underlined words *azure world* most likely refer?
   a. a forest
   b. the sky
   c. the cliff
   d. nature

331. In the second stanza, first line, to which of the following does the verb *crawls* refer?
   a. waves
   b. sunlight on the water
   c. the eagle's prey
   d. the eagle itself

This poem, by Emily Dickinson, is a sort of riddle. Depending on your life experiences, the answer may be immediately clear. Or it may very well not be. Look closely for clues in the language.

A Narrow Fellow in the Grass

A narrow Fellow in the grass
Occasionally rides—
You may have met him—did you not
His notice sudden is—
The Grass divides as with a Comb—
A spotted shaft is seen—
And then it closes at your feet
And opens further on—
He likes a Boggy Acre—
A Floor too cool for Corn—
Yet when a Boy, and Barefoot—
I more than once at Noon
Have passed, I thought, a Whip-lash
Unbraiding in the Sun—
When, stooping to secure it,
It wrinkled, and was gone—

Several of Nature's People
I know, and they know me—
I feel for them a transport
Of cordiality—
But never met this Fellow,
Attended, or alone—
Without a tighter breathing
And zero at the bone—

332. Who or what is the *Fellow* in this poem?
   a. a whip-lash
   b. a snake
   c. a gust of wind
   d. a boy

333. The phrase *Without a tighter breathing / And zero at the bone* most nearly indicates
   a. fright.
   b. cold.
   c. grief.
   d. awe.

334. The phrase *Nature's People* means
   a. nature-lovers.
   b. children.
   c. animals.
   d. neighbors.

335. The speaker of this poem is most likely
   a. an adult woman.
   b. an adult man.
   c. Emily Dickinson, the poet.
   d. a young boy.

It's true that poems often have two levels—one literal, one figurative. The next two poems, also by Emily Dickinson, are full of images from nature. In exploring the second level of meaning, consider the speaker's attitude, revealed especially through surprising, and jarring, word choices.

Apparently with No Surprise

Apparently with no surprise
To any happy flower,
The frost beheads it at its play
In accidental power.

The blond assassin passes on,
The sun proceeds unmoved
To measure off another day
For an approving God.

336. Which of the following most nearly describes the author's attitude toward nature as expressed in this poem?
   a. delight
   b. dismay
   c. indifference
   d. reverence

337. The poem implies that the attitude of the flowers toward the frost is one of
   a. fear.
   b. horror.
   c. acceptance.
   d. reverence.

338. The tone of the poem implies that the speaker probably regards God as
   a. benevolent.
   b. just.
   c. cruel.
   d. angry.

Because I Could Not Stop for Death

Because I could not stop for Death—
He kindly stopped for me—
The carriage held but just Ourselves—
And Immortality.

We slowly drove—He knew no haste,
And I had put away
My labour, and my leisure too,
For His Civility—

We passed the School, where children played
At Recess—in the Ring—
We passed the fields of gazing grain—
We passed the Setting Sun.

We paused before a house that seemed
A swelling of the ground—
The roof was scarcely visible—
The cornice but a mound.

Since then—'tis centuries; but each
Feels shorter than the Day
I first surmised the Horses' Heads
Were toward Eternity—

339. The image of death presented in stanza 1 is that of
  a. an indifferent driver.
  b. a kindly gentleman.
  c. an immortal god disguised as a human.
  d. none of the above.

340. The main idea of the poem is that
  a. death kidnaps its victims and drives away emotionlessly.
  b. death is dull; its chief torment is boredom.
  c. death is a gentle timeless journey, simply leaving life's cares behind.
  d. death is an eternity.

341. In stanza 2, the word *haste* can be defined as
  a. sorrow.
  b. hurry.
  c. guilt.
  d. emotion.

342. The image described in stanza 4 most closely represents
  a. a blurring of life and death.
  b. an inability of the dead to focus on the world of the living.
  c. a description of the grave.
  d. a last image of security one sees before one dies.

343. One can infer from the tone of the poem that the speaker
  a. views Death as a pleasant companion.
  b. views Death as an intruder.
  c. views Death as a figure of authority.
  d. views Death as an intimate friend.

This next poem is by William Shakespeare.

The Seven Ages of Man

All the world's a stage,
And all the men and women merely players;
They have their exits and their entrances;
And one man in his time plays many parts.
His acts being seven ages. At first the infant,
Mewling . . . in the nurse's arms.
And then the whining schoolboy, with his satchel
And shining morning face . . . And then the lover,
Sighing like a furnace . . . Then a soldier
Full of strange oaths . . . Jealous of honor,
Sudden and quick in quarrel . . . And then the
     justice . . .
Full of wise saws and modern instances;
And so he plays his part. The sixth age shifts
Into the lean and slippered pantaloon.
With spectacles on nose and pouch on side.
 . . . and his big manly voice, Turning again toward
Childish treble, pipes and whistles in his sound.
Last scene of all,
That ends this strange eventful history,
Is second childishness, and mere oblivion,
Sans teeth, sans eyes, sans taste, sans everything.

344. What attitude does the speaker reveal by using
the word *merely* in the second line?
a. sorrow
b. anger
c. amusement
d. indifference

345. What characterizes the period of life repre-
sented by the soldier?
a. brash behavior
b. his sense of honor
c. his dedication to duty
d. his fear of cowardice

346. What is the main idea of this poem?
a. Life is a misery that never gets any better at
any time.
b. Life is what each of us makes of it during
our journey down the river of eternity.
c. Life is a play and it follows a specific script,
none of which should cause anguish or
sorrow.
d. Life is a comedy, and we are all buffoons in
pantaloons no matter what we do.

347. What is the theme of the poem?
a. Death is to be feared.
b. Life is a circle that brings us back to the
beginning.
c. The male of the species is the only true
measure of the stages of life.
d. The stages of life are unrelated and can be
altered by each individual's free will.

348. The poet uses the words *merely* (line 2) and
mere (line 20)
a. to soften the effect of the strong images he
presents to us in those lines.
b. to tie together his theme of the cycle of life.
c. convey his tone to the reader.
d. all of the above.

▶ Philosophy and Literature

The next passages are based on philosophy and literature. You don't have to be an expert in either subject to answer the questions correctly. All the information you need is in the passage. Look for the main idea, words in context, and the topic sentence to help you understand the basic information. Then use your ability to make inferences based on the facts in the passage. Using all the available information in the passage will help you identify ideas not explicitly stated in the text.

The answers to this section begin on page 149.

The fictional world of Nobel Prize winner Toni Morrison's novel *Sula*—the African-American section of Medallion, Ohio, a community called the Bottom—is a place where people and natural things are apt to go awry, to break from their prescribed boundaries, a place where bizarre and unnatural happenings and strange reversals of the ordinary are commonplace. The very naming of the setting of *Sula* is a turning upside-down of the expected; the Bottom is located high in the hills. The novel is filled with images of mutilation, both psychological and physical. A great part of the lives of the characters, therefore, is taken up with making sense of the world, setting boundaries, and devising methods to control what is essentially uncontrollable. One of the major devices used by the people of the Bottom is the seemingly universal one of creating a _____; in this case, the title character Sula—upon which to project both the evil they perceive outside themselves and the evil in their own hearts.

349. Which of the following words would best fit into the blank in the final sentence of the passage?
   a. scapegoat
   b. hero
   c. leader
   d. victim

350. Based on the description of the setting of the novel *Sula*, which of the following adjectives would most likely describe the behavior of many of its residents?
   a. furtive
   b. suspicious
   c. unkempt
   d. eccentric

Don't forget to look for the author's attitude in the material you read. Is it positive, negative, or neutral? Ask yourself, how might the author have spoken if he or she had felt differently?

The English language premiere of Samuel Beckett's play *Waiting for Godot* took place in London in August 1955. *Godot* is an avant-garde play with only five characters (not including Mr. Godot, who never arrives) and a minimal setting: one rock and one bare tree. The play has two acts; the second act repeats what little action occurs in the first with few changes: The tree, for instance, acquires one leaf. In a statement that was to become famous, the critic, Vivian Mercer, has described *Godot* as "a play in which nothing happens twice." Opening night, critics and playgoers greeted the play with bafflement and derision. The line, "Nothing happens, nobody comes, nobody goes. It's awful," was met by a loud rejoinder of "Hear! Hear!" from an audience member.

_____.

However, Harold Hobson's review in *The Sunday Times* managed to recognize the play for what history has proven it to be, a revolutionary moment in theater.

351. Which sentence, if inserted in the blank space on the previous page, would make the best sense in the context of the passage?

a. The director, Peter Hall, had to beg the theater management not to close the play immediately but to wait for the Sunday reviews.

b. Despite the audience reaction, the cast and director believed in the play.

c. It looked as if *Waiting for Godot* was beginning a long run as the most controversial play of London's 1955 season.

d. *Waiting for Godot* was in danger of closing the first week of its run and of becoming nothing more than a footnote in the annals of the English stage.

352. Judging from the information provided in the paragraph, which of the following statements is accurate?

a. The 1955 production of *Waiting for Godot* was the play's first performance.

b. *Waiting for Godot* was written by Peter Hall.

c. The sets and characters in *Waiting for Godot* were typical of London stage productions in the 1950s.

d. *Waiting for Godot* was not first performed in English.

353. Which of the following provides the best definition of the term *avant-garde* as the author intends it in the passage?

a. innovative

b. unintelligible

c. foreign

d. high-brow

354. Which of the following best describes the attitude of the author of the passage toward the play *Waiting for Godot*?

a. It was a curiosity in theater history.

b. It is the most important play of the twentieth century.

c. It is too repetitious.

d. It represents a turning point in stage history.

In his famous study of myth, *The Hero with a Thousand Faces*, Joseph Campbell writes about the archetypal hero who has ventured outside the boundaries of the village and, after many trials and adventures, has returned with the <u>boon</u> that will save or enlighten his fellows. Like Carl Jung, Campbell believes that the story of the hero is part of the collective unconscious of all humankind. He likens the returning hero to the sacred or tabooed personage described by James Frazier in *The Golden Bough*. Such an individual must, in many instances of myth, be insulated from the rest of society, "not merely for his own sake but for the sake of others; for since the virtue of holiness is, so to say, a powerful explosive which the smallest touch can detonate, it is necessary in the interest of the general safety to keep it within narrow bounds."

There is _____ between the archetypal hero who has journeyed into the wilderness and the poet who has journeyed into the realm of imagination. Both places are dangerous and full of wonders, and both, at their deepest levels, are journeys that take place in the kingdom of the unconscious mind, a place that, in Campbell's words, "goes down into unsuspected Aladdin caves. There are not only jewels but dangerous jinn abide . . ."

355. The phrase that would most accurately fit into the blank in the first sentence of the second paragraph is
   a. much similarity.
   b. a wide gulf.
   c. long-standing conflict.
   d. an abiding devotion.

356. The title of Campbell's book, *The Hero with a Thousand Faces*, is meant to convey
   a. the many villagers whose lives are changed by the story the hero has to tell.
   b. the fact that the hero journeys into many different imaginary countries.
   c. the many languages into which the myth of the hero has been translated.
   d. the universality of the myth of the hero who journeys into the wilderness.

357. Based on the passage, which of the following best describes the story that will likely be told by Campbell's returning hero and Frazier's sacred or tabooed personage?
   a. a radically mind-altering story
   b. a story that will terrify people to no good end
   c. a warning of catastrophe to come
   d. a story based on a dangerous lie

358. Which of the following is the most accurate definition of the underlined word *boon* as the word is used in the passage?
   a. gift
   b. blessing
   c. charm
   d. prize

359. Based on the passage, which of the following would best describe the hero's journey?
   a. wonderful
   b. terrifying
   c. awesome
   d. whimsical

360. As depicted in the last sentence of the passage, "Aladdin caves" are most likely to be found in
   a. holy books.
   b. fairy tales.
   c. the fantasies of the hero.
   d. the unconscious mind.

This is an excerpt from Mark Twain's short story "Roughing It." Twain gives an eye-witness account of the operation of The Pony Express, the West's first mail system.

The little flat mail-pockets strapped under the rider's thighs would each hold about the bulk of a child's primer. They held many an important business chapter and newspaper letter, but these were written on paper as airy and thin as gold-leaf, nearly, and thus bulk and weight were economized. The stagecoach traveled about a hundred to a hundred and twenty-five miles a day (twenty-four hours), the pony-rider about two hundred and fifty. There were about eighty pony-riders in the saddle all the time, night and day, stretching in a long, scattering procession from Missouri to California, 40 flying eastward, and 40 toward the west, and among them making 400 gallant horses earn a stirring livelihood and see a deal of scenery every single day in the year.

We had a consuming desire, from the beginning, to see a pony-rider, but somehow or other all that passed us and all that met us managed to streak by in the night, and so we heard only a whiz and a hail, and the swift phantom of the desert was gone before we could get our heads out of the windows. But now we were expecting one along every moment, and would see him in broad daylight. Presently the driver exclaims:

"HERE HE COMES!"

Every neck is stretched further, and every eye strained wider. Away across the endless dead level of the prairie a black speck appears against the sky, and it is plain that it moves. Well, I should think so! In a second or two it becomes a horse and rider, rising and falling, rising and falling, rising and falling—sweeping toward us nearer and nearer—growing more and more distinct, more and more sharply defined—nearer and still nearer, and the flutter of the hoofs comes faintly to the ear—another instant a whoop and a hurrah from our upper deck, a wave of the rider's hand, but no reply, and a man and a horse burst past our excited faces, and go swinging away like a belated fragment of a storm!

361. Based on the tone of the passage, which of the following words best describes the author's attitude toward The Pony Express rider?
   a. indifference
   b. fear
   c. bewilderment
   d. excitement

362. The sighting of the pony-rider is told from which viewpoint?
   a. a person sitting on a porch
   b. a passenger inside a stagecoach
   c. a passenger in a hot air balloon
   d. a person picnicking

363. The reader can infer that the stagecoach in the passage did NOT
   a. carry mail.
   b. have windows.
   c. travel by night.
   d. travel a different route from that of The Pony Express.

364. Which of the following is not supported by the passage?
   a. The mail was strapped in a pouch under the rider's thighs.
   b. The rider rode great distances to deliver the mail.
   c. People did not care about The Pony Express rider.
   d. Usually eighty pony riders were in the saddle at any given time.

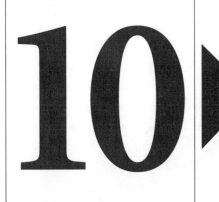

SECTION

10 ▶ Longer Passages

The passages in this section are the final test of your reading comprehension skills. They test your ability to read large blocks of text, define words in context, and respond to questions about content.

You'll find that the longer passages in this section are the most difficult of all the ones you have read in this book so far, but at this point, *you are more than ready* for them. Some of the passages are about new research, geology, history, and even Greek mythology. Some of the passages contain technical and scientific information, much of it related to medicine. If the material looks daunting because of unfamiliar vocabulary, read the passage in a relaxed manner to get a sense of its overall meaning and organizational pattern. After that, go back and read the passage one paragraph at a time. The material will seem less overwhelming if you consider it in smaller chunks. Notes or outlines may also help clarify the material for you.

Remember that the reading process is the same whether the text is long or short, complex or simple, and the way to respond to the questions correctly is to read closely and carefully.

The answers to this section begin on page 150.

The coast of the state of Maine is one of the most irregular in the world. A straight line running from the southernmost coastal city to the northernmost coastal city would measure about 225 miles. If you followed the coastline between these points, you would travel more than ten times as far. This irregularity is the result of what is called a drowned coastline. The term comes from the glacial activity of the ice age. At that time, the whole area that is now Maine was part of a mountain range that towered above the sea. As the glacier descended, however, it expended enormous force on those mountains, and they sank into the sea.

As the mountains sank, ocean water charged over the lowest parts of the remaining land, forming a series of twisting inlets and lagoons of contorted grottos and nooks. The highest parts of the former mountain range, nearest the shore, remained as islands. Mt. Desert Island is one of the most famous of all the islands left behind by the glacier. Marine fossils found here were 225 feet above sea level, indicating the level of the shoreline prior to the glacier.

The 2,500-mile-long rocky and jagged coastline of Maine keeps watch over nearly two thousand islands. Many of these islands are tiny and uninhabited, but many are home to thriving communities. Mt. Desert Island is one of the largest, most beautiful of the Maine coast islands. Measuring 16 miles by 12 miles, Mt. Desert was essentially formed as two distinct islands. It is split almost in half by Somes Sound, a deep and narrow stretch of water, seven miles long.

For years, Mt. Desert Island, particularly its major settlement, Bar Harbor, afforded summer homes for the wealthy. Recently though, Bar Harbor has become a burgeoning arts community as well. But, the best part of the island is the unspoiled forest land known as Acadia National Park. Because the island sits on the boundary line between the temperate and sub-Arctic zones, the island supports the flora and fauna of both zones as well as beach, inland, and alpine plants. It also lies in a major bird migration lane and is a resting spot for many birds. The establishment of Acadia National Park in 1916 means that this natural reserve will be perpetually available to all people, not just the wealthy. Visitors to Acadia may receive nature instruction from the park naturalists as well as enjoy camping, hiking, cycling, and boating. Or they may choose to spend time at the archeological museum, learning about the Stone Age inhabitants of the island.

The best view on Mt. Desert Island is from the top of Cadillac Mountain. This mountain rises 1,532 feet, making it the highest mountain on the Atlantic seaboard. From the summit, you can gaze back toward the mainland or out over the Atlantic Ocean and contemplate the beauty created by a retreating glacier.

365. Which of the following lists of topics best outlines the information in the selection?
  a. Ice-age glacial activity
     The Islands of Casco Bay
     Formation of Cadillac Mountain
     Summer residents of Mt. Desert Island
  b. Formation of a drowned coastline
     The topography of Mt. Desert Island
     The environment of Mt. Desert Island
     Tourist attractions on Mt. Desert Island
  c. Mapping the Maine coastline
     The arts community at Bar Harbor
     History of the National Park System
     Climbing Cadillac Mountain
  d. The effect of glaciers on small islands
     Stone-age dwellers on Mt. Desert Island
     The importance of biodiversity
     Hiking in Acadia National Park

366. Which of the following statements best expresses the main idea of the fourth paragraph of the selection?
  a. The wealthy residents of Mt. Desert Island selfishly kept it to themselves.
  b. Acadia National Park is one of the smallest of the national parks.
  c. On Mt. Desert Island, there is great tension between the year-round residents and the summer tourists.
  d. Due to its location and environment, Mt. Desert Island supports an incredibly diverse animal and plant life.

367. According to the selection, the large number of small islands along the coast of Maine are the result of
  a. glaciers forcing a mountain range into the sea.
  b. Maine's location between the temperate and sub-Arctic zones.
  c. the irregularity of the Maine coast.
  d. the need for summer communities for wealthy tourists and artists.

368. The content of the fourth paragraph indicates that the writer believes that
  a. the continued existence of national parks is threatened by budget cuts.
  b. the best way to preserve the environment on Mt. Desert Island is to limit the number of visitors.
  c. national parks allow large numbers of people to visit and learn about interesting wilderness areas.
  d. Mt. Desert Island is the most interesting tourist attraction in Maine.

369. According to the selection, the coast of Maine is
  a. 2,500 miles long.
  b. 3,500 miles long.
  c. 225 miles long.
  d. 235 miles long.

Today, bicycles are elegantly simple machines that are common around the world. Many people ride bicycles for recreation, whereas others use them as a means of transportation. The first bicycle, called a *draisienne*, was invented in Germany in 1818 by Baron Karl de Drais de Sauerbrun. Because it was made of wood, the *draisienne* wasn't very durable nor did it have pedals. Riders moved it by pushing their feet against the ground.

In 1839, Kirkpatrick Macmillan, a Scottish blacksmith, invented a much better bicycle. Macmillan's machine had tires with iron rims to keep them from getting worn down. He also used foot-operated cranks, similar to pedals, so his bicycle could be ridden at a quick pace. It didn't look much like the modern bicycle, though, because its back wheel was substantially larger than its front wheel. Although Macmillan's bicycles could be ridden easily, they were never produced in large numbers.

In 1861, Frenchman Pierre Michaux and his brother Ernest invented a bicycle with an improved crank mechanism. They called their bicycle a *vélocipède*, but most people called it a "bone shaker" because of the jarring effect of the wood and iron frame. Despite the unflattering nickname, the *vélocipède* was a hit. After a few years, the Michaux family was making hundreds of the machines annually, mostly for fun-seeking young people.

Ten years later, James Starley, an English inventor, made several innovations that <u>revolutionized</u> bicycle design. He made the front wheel many times larger than the back wheel, put a gear on the pedals to make the bicycle more efficient, and lightened the wheels by using wire spokes. Although this bicycle was much lighter and less tiring to ride, it was still clumsy, extremely top-heavy, and ridden mostly for entertainment.

It wasn't until 1874 that the first truly modern bicycle appeared on the scene. Invented by another Englishman, H.J. Lawson, the safety bicycle would look familiar to today's cyclists. The safety bicycle had equal-sized wheels, which made it much less prone to toppling over. Lawson also attached a chain to the pedals to drive the rear wheel. By 1893, the safety bicycle had been further improved with air-filled rubber tires, a diamond-shaped frame, and easy braking. With the improvements provided by Lawson, bicycles became extremely popular and useful for transportation. Today, they are built, used, and enjoyed all over the world.

370. There is enough information in this passage to show that
   a. several people contributed to the development of the modern bicycle.
   b. only a few *vélocipèdes* built by the Michaux family are still in existence.
   c. for most of the nineteenth century, few people rode bicycles just for fun.
   d. bicycles with wheels of different sizes cannot be ridden easily.

371. The first person to use a gear system on bicycles was
  a. H.J. Lawson.
  b. Kirkpatrick Macmillan.
  c. Pierre Michaux.
  d. James Starley.

372. This passage was most likely written in order to
  a. persuade readers to use bicycles for transportation.
  b. describe the problems that bicycle manufacturers encounter.
  c. compare bicycles used for fun with bicycles used for transportation.
  d. tell readers a little about the history of the bicycle.

373. Macmillan added iron rims to the tires of his bicycle to
  a. add weight to the bicycle.
  b. make the tires last longer.
  c. make the ride less bumpy.
  d. make the ride less tiring.

374. Read the following sentence from the fourth paragraph:

Ten years later, James Starley, an English inventor, made several innovations that <u>revolutionized</u> bicycle design.

As it is used in the sentence, the underlined word *revolutionized* most nearly means
  a. cancelled.
  b. changed drastically.
  c. became outdated.
  d. exercised control over.

375. Which of the following statements from the passage represents the writer's *opinion*?
  a. The safety bicycle would look familiar to today's cyclists.
  b. Two hundred years ago, bicycles didn't even exist.
  c. The Michaux brothers called their bicycle a *vélocipède*.
  d. Macmillan's machine had tires with iron rims.

One of the most hazardous conditions a firefighter will ever encounter is a backdraft (also known as a smoke explosion). A backdraft can occur in the hot-smoldering phase of a fire when burning is incomplete and there is not enough oxygen to sustain the fire. Unburned carbon particles and other flammable products, combined with the intense heat, may cause instantaneous combustion if more oxygen reaches the fire.

Firefighters should be aware of the conditions that indicate the possibility for a backdraft to occur. When there is a lack of oxygen during a fire, the smoke becomes filled with carbon dioxide or carbon monoxide and turns dense gray or black. Other warning signs of a potential backdraft are little or no visible flame, excessive heat, smoke leaving the building in puffs, muffled sounds, and smoke-stained windows.

Proper ventilation will make a backdraft less likely. Opening a room or building at the highest point allows heated gases and smoke to be released gradually. However, suddenly breaking a window or opening a door is a mistake, because it allows oxygen to rush in, causing an explosion.

376. A backdraft is a dangerous condition for firefighters mainly because
   a. there is not enough oxygen for breathing.
   b. the heat is extremely intense.
   c. the smoke is dangerously thick.
   d. an explosion occurs.

377. Which of the following is NOT mentioned as a potential backdraft warning sign?
   a. windows stained with smoke
   b. flames shooting up from the building
   c. puffs of smoke leaving the building
   d. more intense heat than usual

378. To prevent the possibility of a backdraft, a firefighter should
   a. carry an oxygen tank.
   b. open a door to allow gases to escape.
   c. make an opening at the top of the building.
   d. break a window to release carbon particles.

379. When compared with a hot, smoldering fire, a fire with visible, high-reaching flames
   a. has more oxygen available for combustion.
   b. has more carbon dioxide available for consumption.
   c. produces more dense gray smoke.
   d. is more likely to cause a backdraft.

The human body can tolerate only a small range of temperature, especially when the person is engaged in vigorous activity. Heat reactions usually occur when large amounts of water and/or salt are lost through excessive sweating following strenuous exercise. When the body becomes overheated and cannot eliminate this excess heat, heat exhaustion and heat stroke are possible.

Heat exhaustion is generally characterized by clammy skin, fatigue, nausea, dizziness, profuse perspiration, and sometimes fainting, resulting from an inadequate intake of water and the loss of fluids. First aid treatment for this condition includes having the victim lie down, raising the feet 8 to 12 inches, applying cool, wet cloths to the skin, and giving the victim sips of salt water (1 teaspoon per glass, half a glass every 15 minutes) over a 1-hour period.

Heat stroke is much more serious; it is an immediate life-threatening situation. The characteristics of heat stroke are a high body temperature (which may reach 106° F or more); a rapid pulse; hot, dry skin; and a blocked sweating mechanism. Victims of this condition may be unconscious, and first-aid measures should be directed at quickly cooling the body. The victim should be placed in a tub of cold water or repeatedly sponged with cool water until his or her temperature is sufficiently lowered. Fans or air conditioners will also help with the cooling process. Care should be taken, however, not to over-chill the victim once the temperature is below 102° F.

380. The most immediate concern of a person tending to a victim of heat stroke should be to
   a. get salt into the victim's body.
   b. raise the victim's feet.
   c. lower the victim's pulse.
   d. lower the victim's temperature.

381. Which of the following is a symptom of heat exhaustion?
   a. unconsciousness
   b. profuse sweating
   c. hot, dry skin
   d. a weak pulse

382. Heat stroke is more serious than heat exhaustion because heat stroke victims
   a. do not sweat.
   b. have no salt in their bodies.
   c. cannot take in water.
   d. have frequent fainting spells.

383. Symptoms such as nausea and dizziness in a heat exhaustion victim indicate that the person most likely needs to
   a. be immediately taken to a hospital.
   b. be given more salt water.
   c. be immersed in a tub of water.
   d. sweat more.

Remember that much scientific and technical writing deals with cold, hard, explicit facts. This means that, with close reading, you stand a good chance of answering most, if not all, of the questions with confidence.

No longer is asthma considered a condition with isolated, acute episodes of bronchospasm. Rather, asthma is now understood to be a chronic inflammatory disorder of the airways—that is, inflammation makes the airways chronically sensitive. When these hyperresponsive airways are irritated, airflow is limited, and attacks of coughing, wheezing, chest tightness, and breathing difficulty occur.

Asthma involves complex interactions among inflammatory cells, mediators, and the cells and tissues in the airways. The interactions result in airflow limitation from acute bronchoconstriction, swelling of the airway wall, increased mucus secretion, and airway remodeling. The inflammation also causes an increase in airway responsiveness. During an asthma attack, the patient attempts to compensate by breathing at a higher lung volume in order to keep the air flowing through the constricted airways, and the greater the airway limitation, the higher the lung volume must be to keep airways open. The morphologic changes that occur in asthma include bronchial infiltration by inflammatory cells. Key effector cells in the inflammatory response are the mast cells, T lymphocytes, and eosinophils. Mast cells and eosinophils are also significant participants in allergic responses, hence the similarities between allergic reactions and asthma attacks. Other changes include mucus plugging of the airways, interstitial edema, and microvascular leakage. Destruction of bronchial epithelium and thickening of the subbasement membrane is also characteristic. In addition, there may be hypertrophy and hyperplasia of airway smooth muscle, increase in goblet cell number, and enlargement of submucous glands.

Although causes of the initial tendency toward inflammation in the airways of patients with asthma are not yet certain, to date the strongest identified risk factor is atopy. This inherited familial tendency to have allergic reactions includes increased sensitivity to allergens that are risk factors for developing asthma. Some of these allergens include domestic dust mites, animals with fur, cockroaches, pollens, and molds. Additionally, asthma may be triggered by viral respiratory infections, especially in children. By avoiding these allergens and triggers, a person with asthma lowers his or her risk of irritating sensitive airways. A few avoidance techniques include: keeping the home clean and well ventilated, using an air conditioner in the summer months when pollen and mold counts are high, and getting an annual influenza vaccination. Of course, asthma sufferers should avoid tobacco smoke altogether. Cigar, cigarette, or pipe smoke is a trigger whether the patient smokes or inhales the smoke from others. Smoke increases the risk of allergic sensitization in children, increases the severity of symptoms, and may be fatal in children who already have asthma. Many of the risk factors for developing asthma may also provoke asthma attacks, and people with asthma may have one or more triggers, which vary from individual to individual. The risk can be further reduced by taking medications that decrease airway inflammation. Most <u>exacerbations</u> can be prevented by the combination of avoiding triggers and taking anti-inflammatory medications. An exception is physical activity, which is a common trigger of <u>exacerbations</u> in asthma patients. However, asthma patients should not necessarily avoid all physical exertion, because some types of activity have been proven to reduce symptoms. Rather, they should work in conjunction with a doctor to design a proper training regimen, which includes the use of medication.

In order to diagnose asthma, a healthcare professional must appreciate the underlying disorder that leads to asthma symptoms and understand how to recognize the condition through information gathered from the patient's history, physical examination, measurements of lung function, and allergic status. Because asthma symptoms vary throughout the day, the respiratory system may appear normal during physical examination. Clinical signs are more likely to be present when a patient is experiencing symptoms; however, the absence of symptoms upon examination does not exclude the diagnosis of asthma.

384. According to the passage, what is the name for the familial inclination to have hypersensitivity to certain allergens?
   a. interstitial edema
   b. hyperplasia
   c. hypertrophy
   d. atopy

385. Why does a person suffering from an asthma attack attempt to inhale more air?
   a. to prevent the loss of consciousness
   b. to keep air flowing through shrunken air passageways
   c. to prevent hyperplasia
   d. to compensate for weakened mast cells, T lymphocytes, and eosinophils

386. The passage suggests that in the past, asthma was regarded as which of the following?
   a. a result of the overuse of tobacco products
   b. a hysterical condition
   c. mysterious, unrelated attacks affecting the lungs
   d. a chronic condition

387. Which of the following would be the best replacement for the underlined word *exacerbations* in this passage?
   a. allergies
   b. attacks
   c. triggers
   d. allergens

388. The passage mentions all of the following bodily changes during an asthma attack EXCEPT
   a. severe cramping in the chest.
   b. heavy breathing.
   c. airways blocked by fluids.
   d. constricted airways.

389. Although it is surprising, which of the following triggers is mentioned in the passage as possibly reducing the symptoms of asthma in some patients?
   a. using a fan instead of an air conditioner in summer months
   b. exposure to second-hand cigarette smoke
   c. the love of a family pet
   d. performing physical exercise

390. Why might a patient with asthma have an apparently normal respiratory system during an examination by a doctor?
   a. Asthma symptoms come and go throughout the day.
   b. Severe asthma occurs only after strenuous physical exertion.
   c. Doctor's offices are smoke free and very clean.
   d. The pollen and mold count may be low that day.

391. Who might be the most logical audience for this passage?
  a. researchers studying the respiratory system
  b. healthcare professionals
  c. a mother whose child has been diagnosed with asthma
  d. an antismoking activist

392. What is the reason given in this article for why passive smoke should be avoided by children?
  a. A smoke-filled room is a breeding ground for viral respiratory infections.
  b. Smoke can stunt an asthmatic child's growth.
  c. Smoke can heighten the intensity of asthma symptoms.
  d. Breathing smoke can lead to a fatal asthma attack.

Millions of people in the United States are affected by eating disorders. More than 90% of those afflicted are adolescents or young adult women. Although all eating disorders share some common manifestations, anorexia nervosa, bulimia nervosa, and binge eating each have distinctive symptoms and risks.

People who intentionally starve themselves (even while experiencing severe hunger pains) suffer from anorexia nervosa. The disorder, which usually begins around the time of puberty, involves extreme weight loss to at least 15% below the individual's normal body weight. Many people with the disorder look emaciated but are convinced they are overweight. In patients with anorexia nervosa, starvation can damage vital organs such as the heart and brain. To protect itself, the body shifts into slow gear: Menstrual periods stop, blood pressure rates drop, and thyroid function slows. Excessive thirst and frequent urination may occur. Dehydration contributes to constipation, and reduced body fat leads to lowered body temperature and the inabil-

ity to withstand cold. Mild anemia, swollen joints, reduced muscle mass, and light-headedness also commonly occur in anorexia nervosa.

Anorexia nervosa sufferers can exhibit sudden angry outbursts or become socially withdrawn. One in ten cases of anorexia nervosa leads to death from starvation, cardiac arrest, other medical complications, or suicide. Clinical depression and anxiety place many individuals with eating disorders at risk for suicidal behavior.

People with bulimia nervosa consume large amounts of food and then rid their bodies of the excess calories by vomiting, abusing laxatives or diuretics, taking enemas, or exercising obsessively. Some use a combination of all these forms of purging. Individuals with bulimia who use drugs to stimulate vomiting, bowel movements, or urination may be in considerable danger, as this practice increases the risk of heart failure. Dieting heavily between episodes of binging and purging is common.

Because many individuals with bulimia binge and purge in secret and maintain normal or above normal body weight, they can often successfully hide their problem for years. But bulimia nervosa patients—even those of normal weight—can severely damage their bodies by frequent binge eating and purging. In rare instances, binge eating causes the stomach to rupture; purging may result in heart failure due to loss of vital minerals such as potassium. Vomiting can cause the esophagus to become inflamed and glands near the cheeks to become swollen. As in anorexia nervosa, bulimia may lead to irregular menstrual periods. Psychological effects include compulsive stealing as well as possible indications of obsessive-compulsive disorder, an illness characterized by repetitive thoughts and behaviors. Obsessive-compulsive disorder can also accompany anorexia nervosa. As with anorexia nervosa, bulimia typically begins during adolescence. Eventually, half of those with anorexia nervosa will develop bulimia. The condition occurs most often in women but is also found in men.

Binge-eating disorder is found in about 2% of the general population. As many as one-third of this group are men. It also affects older women, though with less frequency. Recent research shows that binge-eating disorder occurs in about 30% of people participating in medically supervised weight-control programs. This disorder differs from bulimia because its sufferers do not purge. Individuals with binge-eating disorder feel that they lose control of themselves when eating. They eat large quantities of food and do not stop until they are uncomfortably full. Most sufferers are overweight or obese and have a history of weight fluctuations. As a result, they are prone to the serious medical problems associated with obesity, such as high cholesterol, high blood pressure, and diabetes. Obese individuals also have a higher risk for gallbladder disease, heart disease, and some types of cancer. Usually they have more difficulty losing weight and keeping it off than do people with other serious weight problems. Like anorexic and bulimic sufferers who exhibit psychological problems, individuals with binge-eating disorder have high rates of simultaneously occurring psychiatric illnesses, especially depression.

393. Fatalities occur in what percent of people with anorexia nervosa?
   a. 2%
   b. 10%
   c. 15%
   d. 30%

394. Which of the following consequences do all the eating disorders mentioned in the passage have in common?
   a. heart ailments
   b. stomach rupture
   c. swollen joints
   d. diabetes

395. According to the passage, people with binge-eating disorder are prone to all of the following EXCEPT
   a. loss of control.
   b. depression.
   c. low blood pressure.
   d. high cholesterol.

396. Which of the following is NOT a statement about people with eating disorders?
   a. People with anorexia nervosa commonly have a blood-related deficiency.
   b. People with anorexia nervosa perceive themselves as overweight.
   c. The female population is the primary group affected by eating disorders.
   d. Fifty percent of people with bulimia have had anorexia nervosa.

397. People who have an eating disorder but nevertheless appear to be of normal weight are most likely to have
   a. obsessive-compulsive disorder.
   b. bulimia nervosa.
   c. binge-eating disorder.
   d. anorexia nervosa.

398. Glandular functions of eating-disorder patients slow down as a result of
   a. lowering body temperatures.
   b. excessive thirst and urination.
   c. protective measures taken by the body.
   d. the loss of essential minerals.

399. The inability to eliminate body waste is related to
   a. dehydration.
   b. an inflamed esophagus.
   c. the abuse of laxatives.
   d. weight-control programs.

400. According to the passage, which of the following is true of bulimia patients?
   a. They may demonstrate unpredictable social behavior.
   b. They often engage in compulsive exercise.
   c. They are less susceptible to dehydration than are anorexia patients.
   d. They frequently experience stomach ruptures.

401. Which of the following represent up to two-thirds of the binge-eating disorder population?
   a. older males
   b. older females
   c. younger males
   d. younger females

Greyhound racing is the sixth most popular spectator sport in the United States. Over the last decade, a growing number of racers have been adopted to spend their retirement as household pets, once their racing careers are over.

Many people hesitate to adopt a retired racing greyhound because they think only very old dogs are available. Actually, even champion racers only work until they are about three-and-a-half years old. Because greyhounds usually live to be 12 to 15 years old, their retirement is much longer than their racing careers.

People worry that a greyhound will be more nervous and active than other breeds and will need a large space to run. These are false impressions. Greyhounds have naturally sweet, mild dispositions, and while they love to run, they are sprinters rather than distance runners and are sufficiently exercised with a few daily laps around a fenced-in backyard.

Greyhounds do not make good watchdogs, but they are very good with children, get along well with other dogs (and usually cats as well), and are affectionate and loyal. They are intelligent, well-behaved dogs, usually housebroken in only a few days. A retired racing greyhound is a wonderful pet for almost anyone.

402. Based on the tone of the passage, the author's main purpose is to

a. teach prospective owners how to transform their racing greyhound into a good pet.

b. show how the greyhound's nature makes it equally good as racer and pet.

c. encourage people to adopt retired racing greyhounds.

d. objectively present the pros and cons of adopting a racing greyhound.

403. According to the passage, adopting a greyhound is a good idea for people who

a. do not have children.

b. live in apartments.

c. do not usually like dogs.

d. already have another dog or a cat.

404. Which of the following is implied by the passage?

a. The public is more aware of greyhounds than they used to be.

b. Greyhounds are more competitive than other dogs.

c. Greyhound racing should not be allowed.

d. People who own pet rabbits should not adopt greyhounds.

405. One drawback of adopting a greyhound is that

a. greyhounds are not good with children.

b. greyhounds are old when they retire from racing.

c. the greyhound's sensitivity makes it temperamental.

d. greyhounds are not good watch dogs.

406. This passage is most like an advertisement because it

a. uses statistics to prove its point.

b. does not present information to substantiate its claims.

c. says nothing negative about greyhounds.

d. encourages people to do something.

407. According to the passage, a retired racing greyhound available for adoption will most likely be

a. happy to be retiring.

b. easily housebroken.

c. a champion, or else it would have been euthanized.

d. less high-strung than those that are not available for adoption.

The lives of the Ancient Greeks revolved around *eris*, a concept by which they defined the universe. They believed that the world existed in a condition of opposites. If there was good, then there was evil, if there was love, then there was hatred; joy, then sorrow; war then peace; and so on. The Greeks believed that good *eris* occured when one held a balanced outlook on life and coped with problems as they arose. It was a kind of ease of living that came from trying to bring together the great opposing forces in nature. Bad *eris* was evident in the violent conditions that ruled men's lives. Although these things were found in nature and sometimes could not be controlled, it was believed that bad *eris* occurred when one ignored a problem, letting it grow larger until it destroyed not only that person, but his family as well. The Ancient Greeks saw *eris* as a goddess: Eris, the Goddess of Discord, better known as Trouble.

One myth that expresses this concept of bad *eris* deals with the marriage of King Peleus and the river goddess Thetis. Zeus, the supreme ruler, learns that Thetis would bear a child strong enough to destroy its father. Not wanting to father his own ruin, Zeus convinces Thetis to marry a human, a mortal whose child could never challenge the gods. He promises her, among other things, the greatest wedding in all of Heaven and Earth and allows the couple to invite whomever they please. This is one of the first mixed marriages of Greek Mythology and the lesson learned from it still applies today. They do invite everyone . . . except Eris, the Goddess of Discord. In other words, instead of facing the problems brought on by a mixed marriage, they turn their backs on them. They refused to deal directly with their problems and the result is tragic. In her fury, Eris arrives, ruins the wedding, causes a jealous feud between the three major goddesses over a golden apple, and sets in place the conditions that lead to the Trojan War. The war would take place 20 years in the future, but it would result in the death of the only child of the bride and groom, Achilles. Eris would destroy the parents' hopes for their future, leaving the couple with no legitimate heirs to the throne.

Hence, when we are told, "If you don't invite trouble, trouble comes," it means that if we don't deal with our problems, our problems will deal with us . . . with a vengeance! It is easy to see why the Greeks considered many of their myths learning myths, for this one teaches us the best way to defeat that which can destroy us.

408. According to the passage, the ancient Greeks believed that the concept of eris defined the universe
   a. as a hostile, violent place.
   b. as a condition of opposites.
   c. as a series of problems.
   d. as a mixture of gods and man.

409. Most specifically, *bad* eris is defined in
the passage as
a. the violent conditions of life.
b. the problems man encounters.
c. the evil goddess who has a golden apple.
d. the murderer of generations.

410. It can be inferred that Zeus married Thetis
off because
a. he needed to buy the loyalty of a great king
of mankind.
b. he feared the gods would create bad eris by
competing over her.
c. he feared the Trojan War would be fought
over her.
d. he feared having an affair with her and,
subsequently, a child by her.

411. It can also be inferred that Zeus did not fear a
child sired by King Peleus because
a. he knew that the child could not climb
Mt. Olympus.
b. he knew that the child would be killed in
the Trojan War.
c. he knew that no matter how strong a mortal child was, he couldn't overthrow an
immortal god.
d. he knew that Thetis would always love him
above everyone else.

412. According to the passage, Achilles
a. defeated Zeus during the Trojan War.
b. dies during the Trojan War.
c. was born 20 years after the war because of
the disruption Eris caused at the wedding.
d. was the illegitimate son of Peleus.

413. Which of the following statements is the message offered in the myth?
a. Do not consider a mixed marriage.
b. Do not anger the gods.
c. Do not ignore the problems that arise
in life.
d. Do not take myths seriously.

She was one of those pretty, charming women who are born, as if by an error of Fate, into a petty official's family. She had no dowry,[1] no hopes, nor the slightest chance of being loved and married by a rich man—so she slipped into marriage with a minor civil servant.

Unable to afford jewels, she dressed simply: But she was wretched, for women have neither caste nor breeding—in them beauty, grace, and charm replace pride of birth. Innate refinement, instinctive elegance, and wit give them their place on the only scale that counts, and these make humble girls the peers of the grandest ladies.

She suffered, feeling that every luxury should rightly have been hers. The poverty of her rooms—the shabby walls, the worn furniture, the ugly upholstery caused her pain. All these things that another woman of her class would not even have noticed, made her angry. The very sight of the little Breton girl who cleaned for her awoke rueful thoughts and the wildest dreams in her mind. She dreamt of rooms with Oriental hangings, lighted by tall, bronze torches, and with two huge footmen in knee breeches made drowsy by the heat from the stove, asleep in the wide armchairs. She dreamt of great drawing rooms upholstered in old silks, with fragile little tables holding priceless knickknacks, and of enchanting little sitting rooms designed for tea-time chats with famous, sought-after men whose attentions all women longed for.

She sat down to dinner at her round table with its three-day-old cloth, and watched her husband lift the lid of the soup tureen and delightedly exclaim: "Ah, a good homemade beef stew! There's nothing better!" She visualized elegant dinners with gleaming silver and gorgeous china. She yearned for wall hangings peopled with knights and ladies and exotic birds in a fairy forest. She dreamt of eating the pink flesh of trout or the wings of grouse. She had no proper wardrobe, no jewels, nothing. And those were the only things that she loved—she felt she was made for them. She would have so loved to charm, to be envied, to be admired and sought after.

[1] dowry: property a woman brought to her husband in marriage.

This passage was adapted from "The Necklace," by Guy de Maupassant.

414. Which word best describes the actual living conditions of the couple in the selection?
  a. destitute
  b. poor
  c. comfortable
  d. wealthy

415. Which line best demonstrates the couple's true economic standing?

a. She had no dowry, no hopes, not the slightest chance of being married by a rich man . . .

b. The poverty of her rooms—the shabby walls, the worn furniture, the ugly upholstery caused her pain.

c. She sat down to dinner at her round table with its three-day-old cloth, and watched her husband lift the lid of the soup tureen . . .

d. The very sight of the little Breton girl who cleaned for her awoke rueful thoughts and the wildest dreams in her mind.

416. According to the selection, what can be stated about the marriage of this woman?

a. She married but was ashamed of the insignificant position her husband held.

b. She married on the rebound after a wealthy suitor had abandoned her.

c. She married for love without realizing the consequences to her social standing.

d. She never loved her husband.

417. What can be inferred about the values of both husband and wife?

a. They share the same values.

b. The husband values family and simple comforts of home, whereas his wife views these comforts as cause for her anguish.

c. The husband has ceased to enjoy the simple things and only strives to quench his wife's insatiable desire for luxury.

d. The husband believes that a wholesome meal can solve all problems, while his wife believes it is the presentation of the meal that counts.

418. The main idea of the passage is

a. to have the reader feel great sympathy for the wife.

b. to have the reader feel great sympathy for the husband.

c. to show the class distinctions that were so obvious during the setting of the story.

d. to show the reader how selfish and self-centered the wife is.

419. What part of speech does de Maupassant employ to weave the rich images he presents through the wife's descriptions?

a. adjectives

b. adverbs

c. nouns

d. verbs

Arteries of the heart blocked by plaque can reduce the flow of blood to the heart possibly resulting in heart attack or death. Plaque is actually fat and cholesterol that accumulates on the inside of the arteries. The arteries of the heart are small and can be blocked by such accumulations. There is a medical procedure that creates more space in the blocked artery by inserting and inflating a tiny balloon into the blood vessel. It is called coronary balloon angioplasty. *Angioplasty* means "blood vessel repair." When the balloon is inflated, it compresses the plaque against the wall of the artery, creating more space and improving the flow of blood.

Many doctors choose this technique, because it is less invasive than bypass surgery. Yes, both involve entering the body cavity, but in bypass surgery, the chest must be opened, the ribs must be cut, and the section of diseased artery must be removed and replaced. To replace it, the patient's body is opened, once again, to acquire a healthy section of artery. Usually, this blood vessel is removed from an artery located in the calf of the leg. This means the patient now has two painful incisions that must heal at the same time. There is far more risk in such bypass surgery than in angioplasty, which involves threading a thin tube, called a catheter, into the circulatory system and working it to the damaged artery.

Angioplasty may take between 30 minutes to 3 hours to complete. It begins with a distinctive dye that is injected into the bloodstream. A thin catheter is then inserted into the femoral artery of the leg, near the groin. The doctor monitors the path of the dye using x-rays. He moves the tube through the heart and into the plaque-filled artery. He inflates the balloon, creating more space, deflates the balloon, and removes the tube. It is important to note that the plaque has not been removed; it has just been compressed against the sides of the artery. Sometimes, a *stent* may be implanted, a tiny tube of stainless steel that is expandable when necessary. Its function is to keep the artery open.

There is good news and there is bad news. The good news is that the statistics compiled are superb. Ninety percent of all angioplasty procedures are successful. The risk of dying during an operation of this type is less than 2%. The risk of heart attack is also small: 3–5%. Yet heart surgeons do not take any risk lightly; therefore, a team of surgeons stands ready to perform bypass surgery if needed. The length of hospitalization is only three days. The bad news is twofold. First, this procedure treats the condition but does not eradicate the cause. In 20% of the cases, there is a recurrence of plaque. Second, angioplasty is not recommended for all patients. The surgeons must consider the patient's age, physical history, how severe the blockage is, and, finally, the degree of damage to the artery before they make their determination.

420. When coronary arteries are blocked by plaque, one of the results could be
   a. stroke.
   b. heart attack.
   c. hospitalization.
   d. femoral artery deterioration.

421. According to the passage, angioplasty is
defined as
  a. a tiny balloon.
  b. a plaque-laden artery.
  c. blood vessel repair.
  d. bypass surgery.

422. It can be inferred from the passage that *invasive*
most closely means
  a. entering the body cavity.
  b. causing infection.
  c. resulting in hospitalization.
  d. requiring a specialist's opinion.

423. The angioplasty procedure begins with
  a. a thin catheter being inserted into the
  femoral artery.
  b. a balloon being inflated in the heart.
  c. a special dye being injected into the
  bloodstream.
  d. a healthy artery being removed from the
  calf.

424. It can be inferred from the passage that
  a. a healthy artery is removed and awaits possible bypass surgery.
  b. patients have trouble accepting the idea
  that a tiny balloon will cure the problem.
  c. 3–5% of the patients refuse to undergo
  this procedure.
  d. surgeons do not take even a 2% chance of
  death lightly.

425. Which one of the following statements is true?
  a. The plaque that has caused the problem is
  not removed during angioplasty.
  b. The risk of dying during an angioplasty
  procedure is 3–5%.
  c. The coronary balloon angioplasty is a separate procedure from inflating a balloon into
  a blocked artery.
  d. All of the above statements are true.

The next passages are typical of those you might find in textbooks. The paragraphs are numbered for convenience.

(1) For centuries, time was measured by the position of the sun with the use of sundials. Noon was recognized when the sun was the highest in the sky, and cities would set their clock by this apparent solar time, even though some cities would often be on a slightly different time. Daylight Saving Time (DST), sometimes called summer time, was instituted to make better use of daylight. Thus, clocks are set forward one hour in the spring to move an hour of daylight from the morning to the evening and then set back one hour in the fall to return to normal daylight.

(2) Benjamin Franklin first conceived the idea of daylight saving during his tenure as an American delegate in Paris in 1984 and wrote about it extensively in his essay, "An Economical Project." It is said that Franklin awoke early one morning and was surprised to see the sunlight at such an hour. Always the economist, Franklin believed the practice of moving the time could save on the use of candlelight, as candles were expensive at the time.

(3) In England, builder William Willett (1857–1915) became a strong supporter for Daylight Saving Time upon noticing blinds of many houses were closed on an early sunny morning. Willet believed everyone, including himself, would appreciate longer hours of light in the evenings. In 1909, Sir Robert Pearce introduced a bill in the House of Commons to make it <u>obligatory</u> to adjust the clocks. A bill was drafted and introduced into Parliament several times but met with great opposition, mostly from farmers. Eventually, in 1925, it was decided that summer time should begin on the day following the third Saturday in April and close after the first Saturday in October.

(4) The U.S. Congress passed the Standard Time Act of 1918 to establish standard time and preserve and set Daylight Saving Time across the continent. This act also devised five time zones throughout the United States: Eastern, Central, Mountain, Pacific, and Alaska. The first time zone was set on "the mean astronomical time of the seventy-fifth degree of longitude west from Greenwich" (England). In 1919, this act was repealed.

(5) President Roosevelt established year-round Daylight Saving Time (also called War Time) from 1942–1945. However, after this period, each state adopted its own DST, which proved to be disconcerting to television and radio broadcasting and transportation. In 1966, President Lyndon Johnson created the Department of Transportation and signed the Uniform Time Act. As a result, the Department of Transportation was given the responsibility for the time laws. During the oil embargo and energy crisis of the 1970s, President Richard Nixon extended DST through the Daylight Saving Time Energy Act of 1973 to conserve energy further. This law was modified in 1986, and Daylight Saving Time was reset to begin on the first Sunday in April (to spring ahead) and end on the last Sunday in October (to fall back).

426. As it is used in paragraph 3, the word *obligatory* most nearly means
  a. approved.
  b. sparse.
  c. aberrant.
  d. requisite.

427. Who first established the idea of DST?
  a. President Richard Nixon
  b. Benjamin Franklin
  c. Sir Robert Pearce
  d. President Lyndon Johnson

428. Who opposed the bill that was introduced in the House of Commons in the early 1900s?
  a. Sir Robert Pearce
  b. farmers
  c. television and radio broadcasting companies
  d. the U.S. Congress

429. Which of the following statements is true of the U.S. Department of Transportation?
  a. It was created by President Richard Nixon.
  b. It set standards for DST throughout the world.
  c. It constructed the Uniform Time Act.
  d. It oversees all time laws in the United States.

430. Which of the following would be the best title for this passage?
  a. The History and Rationale of Daylight Saving Time
  b. Lyndon Johnson and the Uniform Time Act
  c. The U.S. Department of Transportation and Daylight Saving Time
  d. Daylight Saving Time in the United States

431. The Daylight Saving Time Energy Act of 1973 was responsible for
  a. preserving and setting Daylight Saving Time across the continent.
  b. instituting five time zones in the United States.
  c. extending Daylight Saving Time in the interest of energy conservation.
  d. conserving energy by giving the Department of Transportation authority over time laws.

(1) Milton Hershey was born near the small village of Derry Church, Pennsylvania, in 1857. It was a _____ beginning that did not foretell his later popularity. Milton only attended school through the fourth grade; at that point, he was apprenticed to a printer in a nearby town. Fortunately for all chocolate lovers, Milton did not excel as a printer. After a while, he left the printing business and was apprenticed to a Lancaster, Pennsylvania candy maker. It was apparent he had found his calling in life, and at the age of eighteen, he opened his own candy store in Philadelphia. In spite of his talents as a candy maker, the shop failed after six years.

(2) It may come as a surprise to current Milton Hershey fans, but his first candy success came with the manufacture of caramel. After the failure of his Philadelphia store, Milton headed for Denver, where he learned the art of making caramels. There he took a job with a local manufacturer who insisted on using fresh milk in making his caramels; Milton saw that this made the caramels especially tasty. After a time in Denver, Milton once again attempted to open his own candy-making businesses, in Chicago, New Orleans, and New York City. Finally, in 1886, he went to Lancaster, Pennsylvania, where he raised the money necessary to try again. This company— the Lancaster Caramel Company—established Milton's reputation as a master candy maker.

(3) In 1893, Milton attended the Chicago International Exposition, where he saw a display of German chocolate-making implements. Captivated by the equipment, he purchased it for his Lancaster candy factory and began producing chocolate, which he used for coating his caramels. By the next year, production had grown to include cocoa, sweet chocolate, and baking chocolate. The Hershey Chocolate company was born in 1894 as a subsidiary of the Lancaster Caramel Company. Six years later, Milton sold the caramel company, but retained the rights, and the equipment, to make chocolate. He believed that a large market of chocolate consumers was waiting for someone to produce reasonably priced candy. He was right.

(4) Milton Hershey returned to the village where he had been born, in the heart of dairy country, and opened his chocolate manufacturing plant. With access to all the fresh milk he needed, he began producing the finest milk chocolate. The plant that opened in a small Pennsylvania village in 1905 is today the largest chocolate factory in the world. The confections created at this facility are favorites around the world.

(5) The area where the factory is located is now known as Hershey, Pennsylvania. Within the first decades of its existence, the town of Hershey thrived, as did the chocolate business. A bank, a school, churches, a department store, even a park and a trolley system all appeared in short order; the town soon even had a zoo. Today, a visit to the area reveals the Hershey Medical Center, Milton Hershey School, and Hershey's Chocolate World—a theme park where visitors are greeted by a giant Reeses Peanut Butter Cup. All of these things—and a huge number of happy chocolate lovers—were made possible because a caramel maker visited the Chicago Exposition of 1893!

432. According to information contained in the passage, the reader can infer which of the following?
   a. Chocolate is popular in every country in the world.
   b. Reeses Peanut Butter Cups are manufactured by the Hershey Chocolate Company.
   c. Chocolate had never been manufactured in the United States before Milton Hershey did it.
   d. The Hershey Chocolate Company now makes more money from Hershey's Chocolate World than from the manufacture and sale of chocolate.

433. Which of the following best defines the word subsidiary as used in paragraph 3?
   a. a company owned entirely by one person
   b. a company founded to support another company
   c. a company that is not incorporated
   d. a company controlled by another company

434. The writer's main purpose in this passage is to
   a. recount the founding of the Hershey Chocolate Company.
   b. describe the process of manufacturing chocolate.
   c. compare the popularity of chocolate to other candies.
   d. explain how apprenticeships work.

435. According to the passage, Milton Hershey sold his caramel company in
   a. 1894.
   b. 1900.
   c. 1904.
   d. 1905.

436. The mention of the Chicago International Exposition of 1893 in the passage indicates that
   a. the exposition in Chicago is held once every three years.
   b. the theme of the exposition of 1893 was "Food from Around the World."
   c. the exposition contained displays from a variety of countries.
   d. the site of the exposition is now a branch of the Hershey Chocolate Company.

437. Which of the following words best fits in the blank in paragraph 1 of the passage?
   a. dramatic
   b. modest
   c. undignified
   d. rewarding

(1) By using tiny probes as neural prostheses, scientists may be able to restore nerve function in quadriplegics and make the blind see or the deaf hear. Thanks to advanced techniques, a single, small, implanted probe can stimulate individual neurons electrically or chemically and then record responses. Preliminary results suggest that the microprobe telemetry systems can be permanently implanted and replace damaged or missing nerves.

(2) The tissue-compatible microprobes represent an advance over the typical aluminum wire electrodes used in studies of the cortex and other brain structures. Researchers accumulate much data using traditional electrodes, but there is a question of how much damage they cause to the nervous system. Microprobes, which are about as thin as a human hair, cause minimal damage and disruption of neurons when inserted into the brain.

(3) In addition to recording nervous-system impulses, the microprobes have minuscule channels that open the way for delivery of drugs, cellular growth factors, neurotransmitters, and other neuroactive compounds to a single neuron or to groups of neurons. Also, patients who lack certain biochemicals could receive doses via prostheses. The probes can have up to four channels, each with its own recording/stimulating electrode.

438. One similar feature of microprobes and wire electrodes is
   a. a minimal disturbance of neurons.
   b. the density of the material.
   c. the capacity for multiple leads.
   d. their ability to generate information.

439. Which of the following best expresses the main idea of the passage?

    a. Microprobes require further technological advances before they can be used in humans.

    b. Wire electrodes are antiquated as a means for delivering neuroactive compounds to the brain.

    c. Microprobes have great potential to help counteract neural damage.

    d. Technology now exists that may enable repair of the nervous system.

440. All of the following are mentioned in the passage as potential uses for prostheses EXCEPT

    a. transportation of medication.

    b. induction of physical movement.

    c. transportation of growth factor.

    d. removal of biochemicals from the cortex.

441. The initial function of microprobe channels is to

    a. create pathways.

    b. disrupt neurons.

    c. replace ribbon cables.

    d. study the brain.

(1) Medical waste has been a growing concern because of recent incidents of public exposure to discarded blood vials, needles (sharps), empty prescription bottles, and syringes. Medical waste can typically include general refuse, human blood and blood products, cultures and stocks of infectious agents, laboratory animal carcasses, contaminated bedding material, and pathological wastes.

(2) Wastes are generally collected by gravity chutes, carts, or pneumatic tubes, each of which has its own advantages and disadvantages. Chutes are limited to vertical transport, and there is some risk of <u>exhausting</u> contaminants into hallways if a door is left open during use. Another disadvantage of gravity chutes is that the waste container may get jammed while dropping, or it may be broken upon hitting the bottom. Carts are primarily for horizontal transport of bagged or containerized wastes. The main risk here is that bags may be broken or torn during transport, potentially exposing the worker to the wastes. Using automated carts can reduce the potential for exposure. Pneumatic tubes offer the best performance for waste transport in a large facility. Advantages include high-speed movement, movement in any direction, and minimal intermediate storage of untreated wastes. However, some objects cannot be conveyed pneumatically.

(3) Off-site disposal of regulated medical wastes remains a viable option for smaller hospitals (those with less than 150 beds). Some preliminary on-site processing, such as compaction or hydropulping, may be necessary prior to sending the waste off site. Compaction reduces the total volume of solid wastes, often reducing trans-

portation and disposal costs, but it does not change the hazardous characteristics of the waste. Compaction may not be economical if transportation and disposal costs are based on weight rather than volume.

(4) Hydropulping involves grinding the waste in the presence of an oxidizing fluid, such as hypochlorite solution. The liquid is separated from the pulp and discharged directly into the sewer unless local limits require additional pretreatment prior to discharge. The pulp can often be disposed of at a landfill. One advantage is that waste can be rendered innocuous and reduced in size within the same system. Disadvantages are the added operating burden, difficulty of controlling <u>fugitive emissions</u>, and the difficulty of conducting microbiological tests to determine whether all organic matters and infectious organisms have been destroyed from the waste.

(5) On-site disposal is a feasible alternative for hospitals generating two tons or more per day of total solid waste. Common treatment techniques include steam sterilization and incineration. Although other options are available, incineration is currently the preferred method for on-site treatment of hospital waste.

(6) Steam sterilization is limited in the types of medical waste it can treat, but is appropriate for laboratory cultures and/or substances contaminated with infectious organisms. The waste is subjected to steam in a sealed, pressurized chamber. The liquid that may form is drained off to the sewer or sent for processing. The unit is then reopened after a vapor release to the atmosphere, and the solid waste is removed for further processing or disposal. One advantage of steam

sterilization is that it has been used for many years in hospitals to sterilize instruments and containers and to treat small quantities of waste. However, since sterilization does not change the appearance of the waste, there could be a problem in gaining acceptance of the waste for landfilling.

(7) A properly designed, maintained, and operated incinerator achieves a relatively high level of organism destruction. Incineration reduces the weight and volume of the waste as much as 95% and is especially appropriate for pathological wastes and sharps. The most common incineration system for medical waste is the controlled-air type. The principal advantage of this type of incinerator is low particulate emissions. Rotary-kiln and grate-type units have been used, but use of grate-type units has been discontinued because of high air emissions. The rotary kiln also puts out high emissions, and the costs have been prohibitive for smaller units.

442. Which of the following organizational schemes is most prevalent in the passage?
   a. chronological order
   b. comparison-contrast
   c. order by topic
   d. hierarchical order

443. One disadvantage of the compaction method of waste disposal is that it
   a. cannot reduce transportation costs.
   b. reduces the volume of solid waste material.
   c. does not allow hospitals to confirm that organic matter has been eliminated.
   d. does not reduce the weight of solid waste material.

444. For hospitals that dispose of waste on their own premises, the optimum treatment method is
   a. incineration.
   b. compaction.
   c. sterilization.
   d. hydropulping.

445. According to the passage, which of the following could be safely disposed of in a landfill but might not be accepted by landfill facilities?
   a. hydropulped material
   b. sterilized waste
   c. incinerated waste
   d. laboratory cultures

446. The two processes mentioned in the passage that involve the formation of liquid are
   a. compaction and hydropulping.
   b. incineration and compaction.
   c. hydropulping and sterilization.
   d. sterilization and incineration.

447. According to the passage, two effective methods for treating waste caused by infectious matter are
   a. steam sterilization and incineration.
   b. hydropulping and steam sterilization.
   c. incineration and compaction.
   d. hydropulping and incineration.

448. Hospitals can minimize employee contact with dangerous waste by switching from
   a. a manual cart to a gravity chute.
   b. an automated cart to a hydropulping machine.
   c. a gravity chute to a manual cart.
   d. a manual cart to an automated cart.

449. The process that transforms waste from hazardous to harmless *and* diminishes waste volume is
   a. sterilization.
   b. hydropulping.
   c. oxidizing.
   d. compacting.

450. The underlined word *exhausting*, as it is used in the second paragraph of the passage, most nearly means
   a. debilitating.
   b. disregarding.
   c. detonating.
   d. discharging.

451. Budgetary constraints have precluded some small hospitals from purchasing
   a. pneumatic tubes.
   b. rotary kilns.
   c. sterilization equipment.
   d. controlled-air kilns.

452. The underlined phrase *fugitive emissions* in the fourth paragraph most nearly means
   a. contaminants that are extremely toxic.
   b. contaminants that are illegally discharged.
   c. contaminants that escape the disposal process.
   d. contaminants that come from micro-biological testing.

Isolate the unfamiliar words as you read, by underlining them or jotting them down. Then go back and look at the sentences before and after them—that is, in their immediate context.

(1) The worst and longest economic crisis in the modern industrial world, the Great Depression in the United States had devastating consequences for American society. At its lowest depth (1932–33), more than 16 million people were unemployed, more than 5,000 banks had closed, and over 85,000 businesses had failed. Millions of Americans lost their jobs, their savings, and even their homes. The homeless built shacks for temporary shelter—these emerging shantytowns were nicknamed Hoovervilles; a bitter homage to President Herbert Hoover, who refused to give government assistance to the jobless. The effects of the Depression—severe unemployment rates and a sharp drop in the production and sales of goods—could also be felt abroad, where many European nations still struggled to recover from World War I.

(2) Although the stock market crash of 1929 marked the onset of the depression, it was not the *cause* of it: Deep, underlying fissures already existed in the economy of the Roaring Twenties. For example, the tariff and war-debt policies after World War I contributed to the instability of the banking system. American banks made loans to European countries following World War I. However, the United States kept high tariffs on goods imported from other nations. These underlined policies worked against one another. If other countries could not sell goods in the United States, they could not make enough money to pay back their loans or to buy American goods.

(3) And while the United States seemed to be enjoying a prosperous period in the 1920s, the wealth was not evenly distributed. Businesses made gains in productivity, but only one segment of the population—the wealthy—reaped large profits. Workers received only a small share of the wealth they helped produce. At the same time, Americans spent more than they earned. Advertising encouraged Americans to buy cars, radios, and household appliances instead of saving or purchasing only what they could afford. Easy credit policies allowed consumers to borrow money and accumulate debt. Investors also wildly speculated on the stock market, often borrowing money on credit to buy shares of a company. Stocks increased beyond their worth, but investors were willing to pay inflated prices because they believed stocks would continue to rise. This bubble burst in the fall of 1929, when investors lost confidence that stock prices would keep rising. As investors sold off stocks, the market spiraled downward. The stock market crash affected the economy in the same way that a stressful event can affect the human body, lowering its resistance to infection.

(4) The ensuing depression led to the election of President Franklin D. Roosevelt in 1932. Roosevelt introduced relief measures that would revive the economy and bring needed relief to Americans suffering the effects of the depression. In his 100 days in office, Roosevelt and Congress passed major legislation that saved banks from closing and regained public confidence. These measures, called the New Deal, included the Agricultural Adjustment Act, which paid farmers to slow their production in order to stabilize food prices; the Federal Deposit

Insurance Corporation, which insured bank deposits if banks failed; and the Securities and Exchange Commission, which regulated the stock market. Although the New Deal offered relief, it did not end the Depression. The economy sagged until the nation entered World War II. However, the New Deal changed the relationship between government and American citizens, by expanding the role of the central government in regulating the economy and creating social assistance programs.

453. The author's main point about the Great Depression is that
   a. government policies had nothing to do with it.
   b. the government immediately stepped in with assistance for the jobless and homeless.
   c. underlying problems in the economy preceded it.
   d. the New Deal policies introduced by Franklin D. Roosevelt ended it.

454. This passage is best described as
   a. an account of the causes and effects of a major event.
   b. a statement supporting the value of federal social policies.
   c. a condemnation of outdated beliefs.
   d. a polite response to controversial issues.

455. The author cites the emergence of Hoovervilles in paragraph 1 as an example of
   a. federally sponsored housing programs.
   b. the resilience of Americans who lost their jobs, savings, and homes.
   c. the government's unwillingness to assist citizens in desperate circumstances.
   d. the effectiveness of the Hoover administration in dealing with the crisis.

456. The term *policies*, as it is used in paragraph 2, most nearly means
   a. theories.
   b. practices.
   c. laws.
   d. examples.

457. The passage suggests that the 1920s was a decade that extolled the value of
   a. thrift.
   b. prudence.
   c. balance.
   d. extravagance.

458. The example of the human body as a metaphor for the economy, which is found at the end of paragraph 3, suggests that
   a. a stressful event like the stock market crash of 1929 probably made a lot of people sick.
   b. the crash weakened the economy's ability to withstand other pressures.
   c. the crash was an untreatable disease.
   d. a single event caused the collapse of the economy.

459. The content in the last paragraph of the passage would most likely support which of the following statements?
   a. The New Deal policies were not radical enough in challenging capitalism.
   b. The economic policies of the New Deal brought about a complete business recovery.
   c. The Agricultural Adjustment Act paid farmers to produce surplus crops.
   d. The federal government became more involved in caring for needy members of society.

(1) The atmosphere forms a gaseous, protective envelope around Earth. It protects the planet from the cold of space, from harmful ultraviolet light, and from all but the largest meteors. After traveling over 93 million miles, solar energy strikes the atmosphere and Earth's surface, warming the planet and creating what is known as the bios-phere, the region of Earth capable of sustaining life. Solar radiation in combination with the planet's rotation causes the atmosphere to circulate. Atmos-pheric circulation is one important reason that life on Earth can exist at higher latitudes because equa-torial heat is transported poleward, moderating the climate.

(2) The equatorial region is the warmest part of the earth because it receives the most direct and, therefore, strongest solar radiation. The plane in which the earth revolves around the sun is called the *ecliptic*. Earth's axis is inclined $23\frac{1}{3}$ degrees with respect to the ecliptic. This inclined axis is responsi-ble for our changing seasons because, as seen from the earth, the sun oscillates back and forth across the equator in an annual cycle. On or about June 21 each year, the sun reaches the Tropic of Cancer, $23\frac{1}{3}$ degrees north latitude. This is the northernmost point where the sun can be directly overhead. On or about December 21 of each year, the sun reaches the Tropic of Capricorn, $23\frac{1}{3}$ degrees south latitude. This is the southernmost point at which the sun can be directly overhead. The polar regions are the coldest parts of the earth because they receive the least direct and, therefore, the weakest solar radiation. Here solar radiation strikes at a very oblique angle and thus spreads the same amount of energy over a greater area than in the equatorial regions. A static envelope of air sur-rounding the earth would produce an extremely hot, uninhabitable equatorial region, while the polar regions would remain inhospitably cold.

(3) The transport of water vapor in the atmosphere is an important mechanism by which heat energy is redistributed poleward. When water evaporates into the air and becomes water vapor, it absorbs energy. At the equator, air satu-rated with water vapor rises high into the atmos-phere where winds aloft carry it poleward. As this moist air approaches the polar regions, it cools and sinks back to earth. At some point, the water vapor condenses out of the air as rain or snow, releasing energy in the process. The now-dry polar air flows back toward the equator to repeat the convection cycle. In this way, heat energy absorbed at the equator is deposited at the poles and the temperature gradient between these regions is reduced.

(4) The circulation of the atmosphere and the weather it generates is but one example of the many complex, interdependent events of nature. The web of life depends on the proper functioning of these natural mechanisms for its continued existence. Global warming, the hole in the atmos-phere's ozone layer, and increasing air and water pollution pose serious, long-term threats to the biosphere. Given the high degree of nature's interconnectedness, it is quite possible that the most serious threats have yet to be recognized.

460. Which of the following best expresses the main idea of the passage?
   a. The circulation of atmosphere, threatened by global warming and pollution, protects the biosphere and makes life on Earth possible.
   b. If the protective atmosphere around the earth is too damaged by human activity, all life on Earth will cease.
   c. Life on Earth is the result of complex interde-pendent events of nature, and some of these events are a result of human intervention.
   d. The circulation of atmosphere is the single most important factor in keeping the bios-phere alive, and it is constantly threatened by harmful human activity.

461. Which of the following best represents the organization of the passage?

  a. I. Definition and description of the circulation of the atmosphere

      II. How the atmosphere affects heat and water in the biosphere

      III. How the circulation of the atmosphere works

      IV. What will happen if human activity destroys the atmosphere and other life-sustaining mechanisms

  b. I. Origin of the atmosphere and ways it protects the biosphere

      II. How the circulation of the atmosphere affects the equator and the poles

      III. How the circulation of the atmosphere interrelates with other events in nature to protect life on Earth

      IV. Threats to life in the biosphere

  c. I. Definition and description of the circulation of the atmosphere

      II. Protective functions of the circulation of the atmosphere

      III. Relationship of the circulation of the atmosphere to other life-sustaining mechanisms

      IV. Threats to nature's interconnectedness in the biosphere

  d. I. The journey of the atmosphere 93 million miles through space.

      II. How the atmosphere circulates and protects the biosphere

      III. How the atmosphere interrelates with weather in the biosphere

      IV. How damage to the biosphere threatens life on Earth

462. Which of the following is the best definition of the underlined word *biosphere* as it is used in the passage?

  a. the protective envelope formed by the atmosphere around the living earth

  b. that part of the earth and its atmosphere in which life can exist

  c. the living things on Earth whose existence is made possible by circulation of the atmosphere

  d. the circulation of the atmosphere's contribution to life on Earth

463. Which of the following sentences from the passage best supports the author's point that circulation of the atmosphere is vital to life on Earth?

  a. The equatorial region is the warmest part of the earth because it receives the most direct and, therefore, strongest solar radiation.

  b. The circulation of the atmosphere and the weather it generates is but one example of the many complex, interdependent events of nature.

  c. [The atmosphere] protects Earth from the cold of space, from harmful ultraviolet light, and from all but the largest meteors.

  d. A static envelope of air surrounding the earth would produce an extremely hot, uninhabitable equatorial region, while the polar regions would remain inhospitably cold.

464. Based on the passage, which of the following is directly responsible for all temperature changes on Earth?
a. variations in the strength of solar radiation
b. variations in the amount of ultraviolet light
c. variation of biologic processes in the biosphere
d. variation in global warming

465. The first paragraph of the passage deals mainly with which of the following effects of the atmosphere on the earth?
a. its sheltering effect
b. its reviving effect
c. its invigorating effect
d. its cleansing effect

(1) There are two types of diabetes, *insulin-dependent* and *non-insulin-dependent*. Between 90–95% of the estimated 13–14 million people in the United States with diabetes have non-insulin-dependent, or Type II, diabetes. Because this form of diabetes usually begins in adults over the age of 40 and is most common after the age of 55, it used to be called adult-onset diabetes. Its symptoms often develop gradually and are hard to identify at first; therefore, nearly half of all people with diabetes do not know they have it. For instance, someone who has developed Type II diabetes may feel tired or ill without knowing why. This can be particularly dangerous because untreated diabetes can cause damage to the heart, blood vessels, eyes, kidneys, and nerves. While the causes, short-term effects, and treatments of the two types of diabetes differ, both types can cause the same long-term health problems.

(2) Most importantly, both types affect the body's ability to use digested food for energy. Diabetes does not interfere with digestion, but it does prevent the body from using an important product of digestion, *glucose* (commonly known as sugar), for energy. After a meal, the normal digestive system breaks some food down into glucose. The blood carries the glucose or sugar throughout the body, causing blood glucose levels to rise. In response to this rise, the hormone insulin is released into the bloodstream and signals the body tissues to metabolize or burn the glucose for fuel, which causes blood glucose levels to return to normal. The glucose that the body does not use right away is stored in the liver, muscle, or fat.

(3) In both types of diabetes, however, this normal process malfunctions. A gland called the *pancreas*, found just behind the stomach, makes *insulin*. In people with insulin-dependent diabetes, the pancreas does not produce insulin at all. This condition usually begins in childhood and is known as Type I (formerly called juvenile-onset) diabetes. These patients must have daily insulin injections to survive. People with non-insulin-dependent diabetes usually produce some insulin in their pancreas, but their bodies' tissues do not respond well to the insulin signal and, therefore, do not metabolize the glucose properly, a condition known as insulin resistance.

(4) Insulin resistance is an important factor in non-insulin-dependent diabetes, and scientists are searching for the causes of insulin resistance. They have identified two possibilities. The first is that there could be a defect in the insulin receptors on cells. Like an appliance that needs to be plugged into an electrical outlet, insulin has to

bind to a receptor in order to function. Several things can go wrong with receptors. For example, there may not be enough receptors to which insulin may bind, or a defect in the receptors may prevent insulin from binding. The second possible cause of insulin resistance is that, although insulin may bind to the receptors, the cells do not read the signal to metabolize the glucose. Scientists continue to study these cells to see why this might happen.

(5) There's no cure for diabetes yet. However, there are ways to alleviate its symptoms. In 1986, a National Institute of Health panel of experts recommended that the best treatment for non-insulin-dependent diabetes is a diet that helps one maintain a normal weight and pays particular attention to a proper balance of the different food groups. Many experts, including those in the American Diabetes Association, recommend that 50–60% of daily calories come from carbohydrates, 12–20% from protein, and no more than 30% from fat. Foods that are rich in carbohydrates, like breads, cereals, fruits, and vegetables, break down into glucose during digestion, causing blood glucose to rise. Additionally, studies have shown that cooked foods raise blood glucose higher than raw, unpeeled foods. A doctor or nutritionist should always be consulted for more of this kind of information and for help in planning a diet to <u>offset</u> the effects of this form of diabetes.

466. According to the passage, what may be the most dangerous aspect of Type II diabetes?
   a. Insulin shots are needed daily for treatment of Type II diabetes.
   b. Type II diabetes may go undetected and, therefore, untreated.
   c. In Type II diabetes, the pancreas does not produce insulin.
   d. Type II diabetes interferes with digestion.

467. Which of the following are the same for Type I and Type II diabetes?
   a. treatments
   b. long-term health risks
   c. short-term effects
   d. causes

468. According to the passage, one place in which excess glucose is stored is the
   a. stomach.
   b. insulin receptors.
   c. pancreas.
   d. liver.

469. A diet dominated by which of the following is recommended for non-insulin-dependent diabetics?
   a. protein
   b. fat
   c. carbohydrates
   d. raw foods

470. Which of the following is the main function of insulin?
　　a. It signals tissues to metabolize sugar.
　　b. It breaks down food into glucose.
　　c. It carries glucose throughout the body.
　　d. It binds to receptors.

471. Which of the following statements best summarizes the main theme of the passage?
　　a. Type I and Type II diabetes are best treated by maintaining a high-protein diet.
　　b. Type II diabetes is a distinct condition that can be managed by maintaining a healthy diet.
　　c. Type I diabetes is an insidious condition most harmful when the patient is not taking daily insulin injections.
　　d. Adults who suspect they may have Type II diabetes should immediately adopt a high-carbohydrate diet.

472. Which of the following is mentioned in the passage as a possible problem with insulin receptors in insulin-resistant individuals?
　　a. Overeating causes the receptors to function improperly.
　　b. There may be an overabundance of receptors present.
　　c. A defect causes the receptors to bind with glucose.
　　d. A defect hinders the receptors from binding with insulin.

473. According to the passage, in normal individuals, which of the following processes occur immediately after the digestive system converts some food into glucose?
　　a. The glucose is metabolized by body tissues.
　　b. Insulin is released into the bloodstream.
　　c. Blood sugar levels rise.
　　d. The pancreas manufactures increased amounts of insulin.

474. Based on the information in the passage, which of the following best describes people with Type I diabetes?
　　a. They do not need to be treated with injections of insulin.
　　b. They comprise the majority of people with diabetes.
　　c. Their pancreases do not produce insulin.
　　d. They are usually diagnosed as adults.

475. What is the closest meaning of the underlined word *offset* in the final sentence of the passage?
　　a. counteract
　　b. cure
　　c. soothe
　　d. erase

(1) The immune system is equal in complexity to the combined <u>intricacies</u> of the brain and nervous system. The success of the immune system in defending the body relies on a dynamic regulatory communications network consisting of millions and millions of cells. Organized into sets and subsets, these cells pass information back and forth like clouds of bees swarming around a hive. The result is a sensitive system of checks and balances that produces an immune response that is prompt, appropriate, effective, and self-limiting.

(2) At the heart of the immune system is the ability to distinguish between self and non-self. When immune defenders encounter cells or organisms carrying foreign or non-self molecules, the immune troops move quickly to eliminate the intruders. Virtually every body cell carries distinctive molecules that identify it as self. The body's immune defenses do not normally attack tissues that carry a self-marker. Rather, immune cells and other body cells coexist peaceably in a state known as *self-tolerance.* When a normally functioning immune system attacks a non-self molecule, the system has the ability to remember the specifics of the foreign body. Upon subsequent encounters with the same species of molecules, the immune system reacts accordingly. With the possible exception of antibodies passed during lactation, this so-called immune system memory is not inherited. Despite the occurrence of a virus in your family, your immune system must learn from experience with the many millions of distinctive non-self molecules in the sea of microbes in which we live. Learning entails producing the appropriate molecules and cells to match up with and counteract each non-self invader.

(3) Any substance capable of triggering an immune response is called an *antigen.* Antigens are not to be confused with *allergens,* which are most often harmless substances (such as ragweed pollen or cat hair) that provoke the immune system to set off the inappropriate and harmful response known as *allergy.* An antigen can be a virus, a bacterium, a fungus, a parasite, or even a portion or product of one of these organisms. Tissues or cells from another individual (except an identical twin, whose cells carry identical self-markers) also act as antigens; because the immune system recognizes transplanted tissues as foreign, it rejects them. The body will even reject nourishing proteins unless they are first broken down by the digestive system into their primary, non-antigenic building blocks. An antigen announces its foreignness by means of intricate and characteristic shapes called *epitopes,* which protrude from its surface. Most antigens, even the simplest microbes, carry several different kinds of epitopes on their surface; some may even carry several hundred. Some epitopes will be more effective than others at stimulating an immune response. Only in abnormal situations does the immune system wrongly identify self as non-self and execute a misdirected immune attack. The result can be a so-called autoimmune disease such as rheumatoid arthritis or systemic lupus erythematosis. The painful side effects of these diseases are caused by a person's immune system actually attacking itself.

476. What is the analogy used to describe the communications network among the cells in the immune system?
   a. the immune system's memory
   b. immune troops eliminating intruders
   c. bees swarming around a hive
   d. a sea of microbes

477. The immune cells and other cells in the body coexist peaceably in a state known as
a. equilibrium.
b. self-tolerance.
c. harmony.
d. tolerance.

478. What is the specific term for the substance capable of triggering an inappropriate or harmful immune response to a harmless substance such as ragweed pollen?
a. antigen
b. microbe
c. allergen
d. autoimmune disease

479. How do the cells in the immune system recognize an antigen as foreign or non-self?
a. through an allergic response
b. through blood type
c. through fine hairs protruding from the antigen surface
d. through characteristic shapes on the antigen surface

480. After you have had the chicken pox, your immune system will be able to do all of the following EXCEPT
a. prevent your offspring from infection by the chicken pox virus.
b. distinguish between your body cells and that of the chicken pox virus.
c. remember previous experiences with the chicken pox virus.
d. match up and counteract non-self molecules in the form of the chicken pox virus.

481. Which of the following best expresses the main idea of this passage?
a. An antigen is any substance that triggers an immune response.
b. The basic function of the immune system is to distinguish between self and non-self.
c. One of the immune system's primary functions is the allergic response.
d. The human body presents an opportune habitat for microbes.

482. Why would tissue transplanted from father to daughter have a greater risk of being detected as foreign than a tissue transplanted between identical twins?
a. The age of the twins' tissue would be the same and, therefore, less likely to be rejected.
b. The identical twin's tissue would carry the same self-markers and would, therefore, be less likely to be rejected.
c. The difference in the sex of the father and daughter would cause the tissue to be rejected by the daughter's immune system.
d. The twins' immune systems would remember the same encounters with childhood illnesses.

483. What is the meaning of the underlined word *intricacies* as it is used in the first sentence of the passage?
a. elaborate interconnections
b. confusion of pathways
c. inherent perplexity
d. comprehensive coverage

(1) An <u>upsurge</u> of new research suggests that animals have a much higher level of brainpower than previously thought. If animals do have intelligence, how do scientists measure it? Before defining animals' intelligence, scientists defined what is not intelligence. *Instinct* is not intelligence. It is a skill programmed into an animal's brain by its genetic heritage. Rote conditioning is also not intelligence. Tricks can be learned by repetition, but no real thinking is involved. *Cuing*, in which animals learn to do or not to do certain things by following outside signals, does not demonstrate intelligence. Scientists believe that insight, the ability to use tools, and communication using human language are all effective measures of the mental ability of animals.

(2) When judging animal intelligence, scientists look for insight, which they define as a flash of sudden understanding. When a young gorilla could not reach fruit from a tree, she noticed crates scattered about the lawn near the tree. She piled the crates into a pyramid, then climbed on them to reach her reward. The gorilla's insight allowed her to solve a new problem without trial and error.

(3) The ability to use tools is also an important sign of intelligence. Crows use sticks to pry peanuts out of cracks. The crow exhibits intelligence by showing it has learned what a stick can do. Likewise, otters use rocks to crack open crab shells in order to get at the meat. In a series of complex moves, chimpanzees have been known to use sticks and stalks in order to get at a favorite snack—termites. To make and use a termite tool, a chimp first selects just the right stalk or twig. He trims and shapes the stick, then finds the entrance to a termite mound. While inserting the stick carefully into the entrance, the chimpanzee turns it skillfully to fit the inner tunnels. The chimp attracts the insects by shaking the twig. Then it

pulls the tool out without scraping off any termites. Finally, he uses his lips to skim the termites into his mouth.

(4) Many animals have learned to communicate using human language. Some primates have learned hundreds of words in sign language. One chimp can recognize and correctly use more than 250 abstract symbols on a keyboard. These symbols represent human words. An amazing parrot can distinguish five objects of two different types. He can understand the difference between the number, color, and kind of object. The ability to classify is a basic thinking skill. He seems to use language to express his needs and emotions. When ill and taken to the animal hospital for his first overnight stay, this parrot turned to go. "Come here!" he cried to a scientist who works with him. "I love you. I'm sorry. Wanna go back?"

(5) The research on animal intelligence raises important questions. If animals are smarter than once thought, would that change the way humans interact with them? Would humans stop hunting them for sport or survival? Would animals still be used for food, clothing, or medical experimentation? Finding the answer to these tough questions makes a difficult puzzle even for a large-brained, problem-solving species like our own.

484. Crows use sticks to pry peanuts out of cracks. Which of the following is the kind of intelligence or conditioning the situation describes?
a. rote learning
b. tools
c. communication
d. instinct

485. The underlined word *upsurge*, as it is used in the first paragraph of the passage, most nearly means
  a. an increasingly large amount.
  b. a decreasing amount.
  c. a well-known amount.
  d. an immeasurable amount.

486. The concluding paragraph of this passage infers which of the following?
  a. There is no definitive line between those animals with intelligence and those without.
  b. Animals are being given opportunities to display their intelligence.
  c. Research showing higher animal intelligence may fuel debate on ethics and cruelty.
  d. Animals are capable of untrained thought well beyond mere instinct.

487. According to the passage, which of the following is true about animals communicating through the use of human language?
  a. Parrots can imitate or repeat a sound.
  b. Dolphins click and whistle.
  c. Crows screech warnings to other crows.
  d. Chimpanzees and gorillas have been trained to use sign language or geometric shapes that stand for words.

488. In paragraph 3, what conclusion can be reached about the chimpanzee's ability to use a tool?
  a. It illustrates high intelligence because he is able to get his food and eat it.
  b. It illustrates instinct because he faced a difficult task and accomplished it.
  c. It illustrates high intelligence because he stored knowledge away and called it up at the right time.
  d. It illustrates high intelligence because termites are protein-packed.

489. Which of the following is NOT a sign of animal intelligence?
  a. shows insight
  b. cues
  c. uses tools
  d. makes a plan

(1) Glaciers consist of fallen snow that compresses over many years into large, thickened ice masses. Most of the world's glacial ice is found in Antarctica and Greenland, but glaciers are found on nearly every continent, even Africa. Presently, 10% of land area is covered with glaciers. Glacial ice often appears blue because ice absorbs all other colors but reflects blue. Almost 90% of an iceberg is below water; only about 10% shows above water. What makes glaciers unique is their ability to move. Due to sheer mass, glaciers flow like very slow rivers. Some glaciers are as small as football fields, whereas others grow to be over 100 kilometers long.

(2) Within the past 750,000 years, scientists know that there have been eight Ice Age cycles, separated by warmer periods called *interglacial* periods. Currently, the earth is nearing the end of an interglacial, meaning that another Ice Age is due in a few thousand years. This is part of the normal climate variation cycle. Greenhouse warming may delay the onset of another glacial era, but scientists still have many questions to answer about climate change. Although glaciers change very slowly over long periods, they may provide important global climate change signals.

(3) The girth of the ice, combined with gravity's influence, causes glaciers to flow very slowly. Once a mass of compressed ice reaches a critical thickness of about 18 meters thick, it becomes so heavy that it begins to deform and move. Ice may flow down mountains and valleys, fan across plains, or spread out to sea. Movement along the underside of a glacier is slower

than movement at the top due to the friction created as it slides along the ground's surface.

(4) Most glaciers are found in <u>remote</u> mountainous areas. However, some found near cities or towns present a danger to the people living nearby. On land, lakes formed on top of a glacier during the melt season may cause floods. At the narrow part of a valley glacier, ice falling from the glacier presents a hazard to hikers below. When ice breaks off over the ocean, an iceberg is formed.

(5) Glaciers are a natural resource and contain 75% of the world's freshwater. People worldwide are trying to harness the power of these frozen streams. Some towns rely on glacial melting from a nearby ice cap to provide drinking water. Some farmers spread soil or ashes over snow to promote melting, hoping that the melting will provide water to irrigate crops in drought-stricken areas. Others have channeled meltwater from glaciers to their fields. Scientists and engineers have worked together to tap into glacial resources, using electricity that has been generated in part by damming glacial meltwater.

490. According to paragraph 4, what is a negative effect of living too close to a glacier?
 a. The mass of the glacier reaches a critical thickness.
 b. About 10% of a glacier shows above water.
 c. Spreading dark material over snow promotes melting.
 d. Lakes formed on top of glaciers may cause floods.

491. The underlined word *remote*, as used in paragraph 4 of the passage, most nearly means
 a. isolated.
 b. nearby.
 c. slow traveling.
 d. difficult to see.

492. The passage explains that glaciers can be found where?
 a. only on Antarctica
 b. only Greenland and Alaska
 c. on nearly every continent
 d. only the north and south poles

493. According to the passage, why does glacial ice often appear blue?
 a. because it does not absorb the color blue
 b. because it absorbs all other colors but reflects blue
 c. because it does not absorb all other colors including blue
 d. because it is blue in color

494. After reading the passage, what can one conclude about glaciers?
 a. There will not be another Ice Age coming.
 b. Glaciers have both negative and positive effects on human life.
 c. Scientists have difficulty studying glaciers.
 d. Scientists have minimal data on the formation of glaciers.

495. After reading the passage, what can one infer about glaciers?
  a. Further exploration is needed to tap the power of glacial ice in fueling electric energy.
  b. With variations in climate, glaciers shrink and expand.
  c. Glaciers form in cold regions where the rate of snowfall is greater than the melting rate of snow.
  d. Glaciers are usually bordered at the sides by rock debris.

(1) A pioneer leader for women's rights, Susan B. Anthony became one of the leading women reformers of the nineteenth century. In Rochester, New York, she began her first public <u>crusade</u> on behalf of temperance. The temperance movement dealt with the abuses of women and children who suffered from alcoholic husbands. Also, she worked tirelessly against slavery and for women's rights. Anthony helped write the history of woman suffrage.

(2) At the time Anthony lived, women did not have the right to vote. Because she voted in the 1872 election, a U.S. Marshall arrested Anthony. She hoped to prove that women had the legal right to vote under the provisions of the fourteenth and fifteenth amendments to the Constitution. At her trial, a hostile federal judge found her guilty and fined her $100, which she refused to pay.

(3) Anthony did not work alone. She collaborated with reformers of women's rights such as Elizabeth Cady Stanton and Amelia Bloomer. Susan worked for the American Anti-Slavery Society with Frederick Douglass, a fugitive slave and black abolitionist. On July 2, 1979, the U.S. Mint honored her work by issuing the Susan B. Anthony dollar coin. Although Anthony did not live to see the fruits of her efforts, the establishment of the nineteenth amendment is indebted to her efforts.

496. What is the main idea of the passage?
  a. Reformers do not always see the results of their efforts.
  b. Susan B. Anthony never gave up her fight for all people's freedoms.
  c. Slavery was one of Susan B. Anthony's causes.
  d. Anthony did not condone the use of alcohol.

497. Anthony advocated all of the following EXCEPT
  a. Slavery should be abolished.
  b. Alcohol should be prohibited because of the abuse it causes.
  c. Women are citizens and should have the right to vote.
  d. Employers should provide child care for female employees.

498. An effective reformer is
   a. a person who has the support of family and friends.
   b. an activist who can enlist the help of others to promote a cause.
   c. a person who is knowledgeable about a particular cause.
   d. a person who ignores what others think.

499. The underlined word *crusade* in paragraph 1 most nearly means
   a. a war against the infidels in the Middle Ages.
   b. a quest to fight evil.
   c. a battle against authority.
   d. a campaign to work tirelessly for one's beliefs.

500. What would historians say was Susan Anthony's greatest achievement?
   a. She collaborated with abolitionists to rid the country of slavery.
   b. She was an activist and raised a family at the same time.
   c. Her tireless efforts to guarantee women the right to vote led to the establishment of the nineteenth amendment to the Constitution.
   d. She was a leader in the temperance movement.

501. In which of the following ways did the U.S. Mint honor her life's work?
   a. The Susan B. Anthony stamp was issued.
   b. The Susan B. Anthony dollar was created.
   c. The Susan B. Anthony Memorial Park was built in Rochester.
   d. Susan B. Anthony dolls were created.

Answers ▶

▶ SECTION 1 Vocabulary

1. c. To be *outmoded* is to be old-fashioned or *out-of-date*. The designer window treatments may also be unnecessary, pointless, or even worthless. However, the key to the meaning is the context—that is, the phrase *installed 17 years ago*.

2. c. Something that is *wearisome* is tiresome or *boring*. The key to the meaning here is the phrase *they regularly put students to sleep*.

3. a. To be *spiteful* is to be vengeful or *vindictive*. The keys here are the word *malice* and the phrase *almost ruined the referee's career*.

4. d. When something is done *obdurately*, it is done in an inflexible or intractable manner, or *stubbornly*. The key here are the words *willful young man*.

5. b. A *superficial* remark is insignificant and shallow, or *petty*. The key here is the word *trivialized*.

6. a. To be *ostracized* is to be banished or *excluded*. The key here is the phrase *usually loyal friends, who had never shunned her before*.

7. b. Something that is *flamboyant* is flashy or *showy*. The keys here are the words *usually described as flamboyant* and *but…uncharacteristically modest*.

8. b. To be *gullible* means to be easy to fool or *naïve*. The keys here are the words *outlandish excuses* and *insincere employees*.

9. a. A *prerequisite* is something that is necessary or *required*. The fact that you can't become a certified teacher without completing the student teaching assignment means that it is required. The other choices do not imply a hard and fast rule.

10. c. To be *diligent* is to be painstaking or *thorough*.

11. d. To be *ambiguous* is to be vague or *unclear*.

12. d. Something that is *animated* is energetic or *lively*.

13. b. When something is *intermittent*, it is *periodic* or starts and stops at intervals.

14. a. To be *diplomatic* is to be sensitive in dealing with others or *tactful*.

15. d. To *augment* something is to add to or *expand* it. Although choice **c**, *consider*, is not out of

131

the question, since officials are responding to several fires that have already occurred, it is more likely that they will do something more pronounced and definitive than just considering the existing rules.

16. d. To be *inundated* is to be overwhelmed or *flooded*.

17. c. To be *unique* is to be one of a kind or *unparalleled*.

18. d. When one is *incredulous*, one is skeptical or *disbelieving*.

19. d. When one is *proficient* at something, one is an expert or is *skilled* at it.

20. a. When something is *tentative,* it is of an uncertain or *provisional* nature.

21. b. When a group's opinion is *unanimous*, it is in accord or *uniform*.

22. a. To *alleviate* something is to make it more bearable or to *ease* it.

23. c. To be *indispensable* is to be necessary or *essential*.

24. a. To *expedite* a process is to hurry it up or *accelerate* it.

25. b. If something is *plausible*, it is believable or *credible*.

26. c. To *infer* something is to *surmise* it or deduce it from the evidence.

27. d. An *ultimatum* is a final statement of terms or *non-negotiable demand*.

28. b. To be *meticulous* is to be extremely careful or *painstaking*.

29. b. To be *apathetic* is to show little or no interest or to be *indifferent*.

30. a. To be *fortified* is to be strengthened or *reinforced*.

31. d. To *delegate* a task is to *assign* it or to appoint another to do it.

32. c. To *arouse* someone is to stir up or *provoke* that person.

33. d. To *articulate* something is to give words to it or *express* it.

34. c. If something is *expansive*, it is broad, open, or *spacious*.

35. b. If a thing is *detrimental*, it is injurious or *harmful*.

36. b. *Crooning* and *bellowing* both mean singing.

37. d. *Fallout* is a side effect that occurs as a result of some incident, action, or happening—that is, it's a *consequence of something*. It is the most logical word to describe something that affects a victim for years.

38. b. *Humid* and *damp* both mean the same thing in this context.

39. b. A *sphere* is a *globular* (*globe*) object.

40. d. To *decontaminate* and to *purify* both mean to remove impurities.

41. c. To be *tailored* and to be *altered* both mean to be made to fit.

42. a. *Dormant* and *inactive* both mean not active, as if asleep (the root meaning of *dormant*).

43. c. To be *banished* and to be *exiled* both mean to be forced to leave.

44. b. *Yielded* and *relinquished* both mean given up.

45. c. A *journal* and a *diary* are both records of daily happenings.

46. b. To be *jostled* is to be *bumped*.

47. a. A *hostel* and an *inn* are both lodging places for travelers.

48. a. *Philosophy* means a system of motivating *principles*.

49. b. The key here is the phrase, *We had no idea who the special guest speaker would be*. This implies there is something hidden or secret. The other choices are unrelated to not knowing who the speaker would be.

50. c. To consider is to think about. The other choices make no sense in the context of the sentence.

51. a. An *opportunity* is a chance. The other choices make no sense in the context of this sentence.

52. b. A *grimace* is a contortion of the face. Neither a *wrinkle* nor a *simper* match the descriptive word *ferocious*. A *shriek* would be described in terms of sound, rather than looks.

53. d. Answers **a** and **c** do not include the sense of hierarchy conveyed in the phrase *to enforce social order*. Answer **b** does convey a sense of hierarchy, but in the wrong order.

54. a. This is the choice that makes the most sense when imagining objects floating in space.

55. b. Although a muscle that atrophies may be *weakened* (choice **c**), the primary meaning of the phrase *to atrophy* is *to waste away*.

56. a. The passage implies that the other women in the orchestra were conventional because of the way they dressed and wore their hair. Because Robin does things differently, she would be considered *unconventional*. The other choices, although she may be joyful, unreliable, and proud, have nothing to do with the context of this sentence, which is directly addressing her appearance as it compares to the other women in the orchestra.

57. a. To depict the Sami, the author uses words that point to their gentleness, which is an admirable quality: They move *quietly*, display *courtesy* to the spirits of the wilderness, and were known as *peaceful retreaters*. There is nothing pitying, contemptuous, or patronizing in the language, and nothing in the passage indicates that the author is perplexed—the description of the Sami is clear and to the point.

58. b. The immediate context of the word *animistic* defines the word: *for [the Sami], nature and natural objects had a conscious life, a spirit*. There is no indication in the passage that the author believes the Sami's animistic religion is *irrational* (choice **a**). The other choices are not in the passage.

59. c. Throughout the passage, the author displays a positive attitude toward the Sami and their beliefs. Although they are said to be *peaceful*, they are not said to be timid or fearful (they retreated from war because they *did not believe* in it). In the context of the passage, it's most likely that the Sami *avoid making a disturbance* in the wilderness out of *respect* for the spirits.

▶ SECTION 2 Analogies

60. b. A petal is *a part of* a flower; a leaf is *a part of* a tree.

61. d. A shelf is *a part of* a bookcase; a key is *a part of* a piano.

62. a. *A group of* fish is called a school; *a group of* wolves is called a pack.

63. a. A scale *measures* weight; a yardstick *measures* length.

64. d. Watermelon is *a kind of* fruit; Dalmatian is *a kind of* canine.

65. e. A foot *propels* a skateboard; a pedal *propels* a bicycle.

66. c. Stretch and extend *are synonyms;* shake and tremble *are synonyms*.

67. c. A kangaroo *is a* marsupial; a rhinoceros *is a* pachyderm.

68. e. Starving is *an intensification of* hungry; depressed is *an intensification of* sad.

69. a. A dermatologist *treats* acne; a psychologist *treats* a neurosis.

70. e. A frame *surrounds* a picture; a fence *surrounds* a backyard.

71. b. One searches *in order to* find; one explores *in order to* discover.

72. c. A pharmacy *sells* drugs; a bakery *sells* bread.

73. a. Layer and tier *are synonyms;* section and segment *are synonyms*.

74. **a.** Metropolitan *describes* urban *areas*; bucolic *describes* rural *areas*.

75. **d.** A teacher *works in a* school; a judge *works in a* courthouse.

76. **c.** A Persian is *a type of* cat; a parakeet is *a type of* bird.

77. **e.** To jog *is to* run *slowly*; to drizzle *is to* rain *slowly*.

78. **c.** A skein is *a quantity of* yarn; a ream is *a quantity of* paper.

79. **b.** To tailor a suit *is to alter it*; to edit a manuscript *is to alter it*.

80. **d.** A conductor *leads an* orchestra; a skipper *leads a* crew.

81. **a.** Jaundice is *an indication of a* liver *problem*; rash is *an indication of a* skin *problem*.

82. **b.** A cobbler *makes and repairs* shoes; a contractor *builds and repairs* buildings.

83. **e.** To be phobic is *to be extremely* fearful; to be ridiculous is *to be extremely* silly.

84. **c.** Obsession is *a greater degree of* interest; fantasy is *a greater degree of* dream.

85. **d.** Devotion is *characteristic of a* monk; wanderlust is *characteristic of a* rover.

86. **e.** Slapstick *results in* laughter; horror *results in* fear.

87. **b.** Verve and enthusiasm *are synonyms*; devotion and reverence *are synonyms*.

88. **c.** A cacophony is *an unpleasant* sound; a stench is *an unpleasant* smell.

89. **a.** A conviction *results in* incarceration; a reduction *results in* diminution.

90. **a.** The deltoid *is a* muscle; the radius *is a* bone.

91. **d.** Umbrage and offense *are synonyms*; elation and jubilance *are synonyms*.

92. **b.** Being erudite is *a trait of a* professor; being imaginative is *a trait of an* inventor.

93. **d.** Dependable and capricious *are antonyms*; capable and inept *are antonyms*.

94. **a.** A palm (tree) *has* fronds; a porcupine *has* quills.

95. **e.** A metaphor *is a* symbol; an analogy *is a* comparison.

96. **d.** A dirge is *a song used at a* funeral; a jingle is *a song used in a* commercial.

97. **e.** Feral and tame *are antonyms*; ephemeral and immortal *are antonyms*.

98. **a.** A spy *acts in a* clandestine *manner*; an accountant *acts in a* meticulous *manner*.

99. **c.** Hegemony *means* dominance; autonomy *means* independence.

100. **e.** An aerie *is where an* eagle *lives*; a house *is where a* person *lives*.

▶ SECTION 3 Main Ideas, Themes

101. **d.** The author stresses the convenience of fitness walking, by stating that it does not require a commute to a health club. The paragraph also implies that fitness walking will result in a good workout. Choice **a** is incorrect because no comparison to weight lifting is made. Choice **b** may seem like a logical answer, but the paragraph only refers to people who are fitness walkers, so for others, a health club might be a good investment. Choice **c** is not in the passage. Although choice **e** seems logical, the paragraph does not indicate that the wrong shoes will produce major injuries.

102. **b.** The last sentence in the paragraph clearly supports the idea that the renewed interest in Shakespeare is due to the development of his characters. Choice **a** is incorrect because the writer never makes this type of comparison. Choice **c** is wrong, because even though scholars are mentioned in the paragraph, there is no indication that the scholars are compiling the anthology. Choice **d** is wrong because there is no support to show that most New Yorkers are interested in this work. There is no support for choice **e** either.

103. **d.** This answer is implied by the whole paragraph. The author stresses the need to read critically by

performing operations on the text in a slow and specific manner. Choice **a** is incorrect because the author never says that reading is dull. Choices **b, c,** and **e** are not supported by the paragraph.

104. a. The support for this choice is in the second sentence, which states that in some countries, toxic insecticides are still legal. Choice **b** is incorrect because even though polar regions are mentioned in the paragraph, there is no support for the idea that warmer regions are not just as affected. There is no support for choice **c**. Choice **d** can be ruled out because there is nothing to indicate that DDT and toxaphene are the most toxic. Choice **e** is illogical.

105. a. The second and third sentence combine to give support to choice **a**. The statement stresses that there must be a judge's approval (i.e., legal authorization) before a search can be conducted. Choices **b** and **d** are wrong because it is not enough for the police to have direct evidence or a reasonable belief—a judge must authorize the search for it to be legal. Choices **c** and **e** are not mentioned in the passage.

106. e. This answer is clearly stated in the last sentence of the paragraph. Choice **a** can be ruled out because there is no support to show that studying math is dangerous. Words are not mentioned in the passage, which rules out choice **b**. There is no support for choice **c**. Choice **d** is a contradiction to the information in the passage.

107. d. The last sentence states that new technologies are reported daily, and this implies that new technologies are being constantly developed. There is no support for choice **a**. With regard to choice **b**, stone tools were first used two and a half million years ago, but they were not necessarily in use all that time. Choice **c** is clearly wrong because the paragraph states when

stone tools first came into use. Although some may agree that choice **e** is true, the author of the paragraph does not give support for this opinion.

108. d. Choices **a** and **c** are not supported by the paragraph. Choices **b** and **e** only tell us about particular parts of the paragraph and are too specific to be the main idea. Choice **d**, however, is general enough to encompass all the sentences and the paragraph as a whole. Every sentence supports the idea asserted in choice **d**.

109. d. Both sentences in the paragraph support this choice. Choices **a** and **e** are opinions and are not in the paragraph. Choices **b** and **c** may be true, but they are also not supported by the paragraph.

110. c. The first sentence points out that it is not practical to use the first-person point of view in business correspondence. Choices **a**, **b**, and **e** are not in the paragraph. Choice **d** is in the paragraph and although it does tell us something about the first-person point of view, it is too narrow to represent the main idea, which has to do with the first-person point of view as it is related to writing in a business environment.

► SECTION 4 Topic Sentences

111. d. The mention that searching for spices has changed the course of history, and that for spices, *nations have . . . gone to war,* implies that the subject of the paragraph is history. These phrases also connote danger and intrigue.

112. c. The mention of all the amazing things the brain is capable of is directly relevant to its being mysterious and complex. The other choices are less relevant.

113. b. Choice **b** addresses both of Gary's vanities: his person and his situation. Choice **a** deals only with one of Gary's physical characteristics. Choice **c** deals only with his vanity of position. Choice **d** is not supported in the passage.

114. a. This choice refers both to age and complexity; **b** and **c** refer only to complexity. Answer **d** is less relevant to the topic sentence (which doesn't mention Darwin or theories) than the other choices.

115. b. This choice is the only one that supports and develops the topic sentence. The other choices all say something about cosmetic plastic surgery, but they do not support the topic sentence, which states that cosmetic plastic surgery is one of the fastest-growing segments of U.S. medicine.

116. c. The topic sentence speaks of the big-bang theory being much misunderstood, and **c** addresses this, whereas the other choices do not.

117. d. Only this choice deals with learning how to accept oneself and then relates it to another person. Choices **a** and **c** are both irrelevant to the topic sentence. Choice **b** states the exact opposite of the topic sentence.

118. c. Choice **c** is the only entry that presents the similar traits of both the hero and the superstar. Choice **a** only defines a superstar. Choice **b** defines the hero. Choice **d** introduces irrelevant material—the sports arena, with no mention of the superstar.

119. a. This choice is a comparison between man and bird. Neither one needs instruction to do what is important to its life. Choices **b, c,** and **d** do not support this topic sentence.

120. b. This choice is the only one that talks about how parents make a difference in their children's academic success. The other choices don't mention parents at all.

121. c. The main idea is that the United States limits immigration numbers. Choices **a, b,** and **d** show the effects and statistics that result from this actio but do not support the topic sentence.

122. d. The topic sentence refers to punishment used in early America. Choice **a** gives a reason for the use of punishment in early America. Choices **b** and **c** state why we don't have such punishment today and compares historical punishment with today's sensibility.

123. d. Choice **d** gives us a reason why more people are eating organic, so it supports the statement made in the topic sentence. Choices **a** and **b** are about organic products, but they don't provide logical reasons for the increasing popularity of organic foods. Choice **c** is about another topic completely.

124. c. This choice introduces the idea that some laws are strange. Choices **a, b,** and **d** are examples of strange laws.

125. a. This topic sentence states the importance of a cat's whiskers. Choices **b, c,** and **d** give other details that do not directly support the topic sentence.

126. c. This choice states the popularity of the game. Choices **a** and **b** state the game's origin. Choice **d** explains how its popularity spread.

127. c. This sentence gives a reason for longevity that was introduced in the topic sentence. Choices **a, b,** and **d** are about longevity but do not give any reasons.

128. a. Choice **a** pronounces an end to 16 years of violence. Choice **b, c** and **d** are facts about James's life.

129. c. Great wealth is not an indicator of honor. Each of the other choices describes the honor that is received. Choice **a** says, greatly respected, choice **b**—a revered poet, and choice **d**—long-lasting reputation.

130. b. The topic sentence presents the idea that all the men are connected by whale lines, each man relies on the others for his safety. Choice **a** states this idea explicitly: Each man "had to depend on the others to stay alive." Choice **c** presents the idea as metaphorical, each man is connected to the next. Choice **d** offers an example of how a man can be thrown overboard and must rely on his crew to cut their whale loose and come back and get him. Only choice **b** does not make any connection to the men.

▶ SECTION 5 Short Passages

131. a. Choice **d** may seem attractive at first, but the passage simply says that the local media does not adequately cover local politics—it doesn't discuss the reason for their neglect.

132. c. Sentence 3 indicates the importance of organization and design. The other choices, even if true, are not in the passage.

133. b. Both sentences in this passage support the idea that the emphasis on the low-carb/low-fat debate is misleading and might distract us from other important ideas. The other choices are not supported by or developed in this passage.

134. b. The other choices are wrong because the passage is not concerned with how sanitation workers should deal with sharp objects but with how everyone should dispose of sharp objects in order to avoid hurting sanitation workers.

135. d. See the second sentence of the passage. Choices **a** and **b** are not in the passage. Choice **c** might seem attractive, but the passage does not say that mediation is the best way to resolve a conflict, simply that it is an alternative way that might prove effective.

136. c. See the final sentence of the passage. The other choices might be true but are not in the passage.

137. a. The second sentence speaks of *the greater productivity* of telecommuters. The other choices may seem attractive on the surface because they contain words and phrases from the passage, but a closer look will show them to be incorrect or absent from the passage.

138. d. The first sentence indicates that sushi was once available only in a handful of eating establishments.

139. c. Choice **b** may seem attractive at first, but the passage doesn't offer the opinion that the purpose of the shopping mall is important, it simply tells us what the purposes are.

140. d. The directions mention nothing about fertilization.

141. c. The third sentence specifically mentions that the pointed side goes up and the root side faces down. This means that there is an up side and a down side and that it is possible for the bulb to be put into the soil upside down if someone didn't know better. The other choices may be true but are not mentioned in the passage.

142. c. The directions indicate that the city *prefers,* but does not require, use of its new container, and that the customers may use more than one container if they purchase an additional one.

143. b. The directions state use of the new containers will *expedite pick-up of recyclables.* This indicates that the new containers will make the recycling program more efficient.

144. b. See the second and third sentences for the steps in making ratatouille. Only choice **b** reflects the correct order.

145. d. The main part of the passage describes how to cook vegetables. Only choice **d** indicates that vegetables are included in the dish. The other choices are not reflected in the passage.

146. d. See the final sentence of the passage.

147. c. See the second sentence, which defines *ksa.* The other choices are refuted in the passage.

148. d. This answer is implied by the statement that redistribution is needed so that people in emerging nations can have proper medical care. Choices **a, b,** and **c** are not mentioned in the passage.

149. c. This choice is the best answer because the paragraph indicates that the new knitters are of varying ages and are not just women. Choices **a** and **b** may be true, but they are not supported by the paragraph. Choice **d** is a prediction that is not made in the paragraph.

150. d. The paragraph specifically states that age makes a person less able to respond to long exposure to very hot or very cold temperatures. This would mean that older people are more susceptible to hypothermia. Choices **a, b,** and **c** are not supported by the information given in the paragraph.

151. c. The third sentence is the main idea. It is a general idea that answers the only question posed in the passage. The other choices are not in the passage.

152. d. The passage states that health clubs have undergone a major transformation due to people's interest in taking care of their minds, bodies, and spirits. Choice **a** is incorrect because the paragraph doesn't say exercise is less important. It simply says the focus and type of exercise have changed. Choices **b** and **c** are not supported by the paragraph.

153. c. This choice is closely related to all three sentences of the passage. Choice **a** is contradicted in the passage. Choices **b** and **d** are not in the passage.

154. a. The entire passage relates to this idea. The other ideas are not reflected in the passage.

155. a. This is the main idea of the passage because all the sentences relate to it. The other choices may be true but are not reflected in the passage.

156. c. This idea is expressed in the final sentence and wraps up the passage, speaking of the importance of *creating a balance*. The other choices are not in the passage.

157. c. The support for choice **c** is given in the second sentence. No support is given for choices **a** and **d**. Choice **b** is incorrect because the paragraph states that women business owners face unique

obstacles, but it does not say that they absolutely require outside help to succeed, just that it is available.

158. d. This choice encompasses the main information in the passage. Choices **a, b,** and **c** are not mentioned.

159. a. The title should express the main idea of the passage. The passage, as a whole, focuses on appropriate and inappropriate uses of e-mail. The other choices address more specific ideas expressed in the passage but are not its *main* idea.

160. c. The first and second sentences reflect this idea. The passage does not say that Native American art is dreamlike (choice **a**). Choices **b** and **d** are too limited to be main ideas.

161. a. This idea is expressed in two of the three sentences in the passage and sums up the overall meaning of the passage.

162. d. This is stated in the final paragraph. The other choices are not reflected in the passage.

163. c. This choice most nearly encompasses the passage and is reflected in the final sentence.

164. b. The passage defines an ecosystem as a community within which all members interrelate. (See the first three sentences of the paragraph.) Choice **a** is only one example of an interaction. The other two choices are too limited to sum up ecosystem activities.

165. b. This is the only choice that reflects the idea of interaction among all members of the group spoken of in the first sentence. The other choices are only physical settings.

166. c. The entire passage supports this idea. Choice **a** is incorrect because the business aspect of alternative medicine is not discussed in the passage. Choices **b** and **d** reflect accurate supporting statements that do appear in the passage, but they are not encompassing enough to reflect the main idea.

167. **a.** Pain management is a generic term and pain management treatment can be alternative or traditional, depending on the practitioner. Choices **b, c,** and **d** are not correct because they are all mentioned in the passage as being particular alternative medicine practices.

168. **a.** The last sentence of the second paragraph clearly states that people born before 1945 are the least likely to turn to alternative therapies.

169. **d.** The beginning of the last paragraph discusses this scientific investigation and its role in making alternative treatments more accepted by mainstream medicine.

170. **b.** See the first paragraph. Choice **a** is contradicted in the first paragraph. Choice **c** is perhaps true but is not in the passage. Choice **d** is incorrect because, although the president's assistant escorted Autherine Lucy to class, the passage does not say that the assistant *befriended* her. Accompanying her to class may just have been his assigned job.

171. **b.** The first paragraph says that Autherine Lucy *bravely* took her seat, and the last paragraph refers to her *courage*.

172. **a.** According to the first paragraph, Autherine Lucy was surprised when the professor apparently did not notice her.

173. **d.** See the fourth sentence of paragraph 2.

174. **c.** The other answers are all contrary to information in the passage.

175. **c.** The passage clearly states this as the reason why Kwanzaa is celebrated.

176. **a.** This is the only correct choice.

177. **d.** The passage does not mention this choice.

178. **d.** This is the definition of Kwanzaa.

179. **d.** Nowhere in the passage is it mentioned that the Spanish outnumbered the Aztecs.

180. **a.** Each statement about Cortez is true, but only this answer matched the prophecy.

181. **d.** The passage explains that Cortez sought gold and created Mexico City.

182. **b.** This choice best captures the theme of the encounter.

183. **a.** The examples in this passage are mainly about Roosevelt's accomplishments.

184. **c.** The second sentence of the first paragraph supports this choice.

185. **b.** In the second paragraph, the first sentence supports this answer.

186. **a.** This is the only choice and is stated in paragraph 1.

187. **b.** This is the only correct choice.

188. **b.** The important part of the question the reader should consider is "the origin of all species." This answer best supports Darwin's theory.

189. **c.** These are the only two principles mentioned in the passage.

190. **b.** Religious opponents condemned his work.

191. **b.** *Six thousand years ago* must account for over 2,000 years after the birth of Christ, and that leaves almost 4,000 years in the B.C. era. All other choices are incorrect math.

192. **b.** The Carib were not in any way described as peaceful but rather, *hostile* people. Therefore, this answer is the exception. All other choices are descriptive of the Caribs and are explicit in the passage.

193. **a.** The last two lines of the passage directly state what defeated the Caribs. Choice **b** is incorrect since the Arawaks were defeated by the Carib, and neither the Dutch nor the French were mentioned in the role of conquerors.

194. **b.** Strife means *war.* Choice **c** refers to the products one can buy on the modern St. Maarten. Choice **d** makes no sense since the time of strife is when the tribe allowed a chief to be chosen. Choice **a** is not mentioned in conjunction with being warlike or with strife; it is added as another characteristic.

195. c. Present-day St. Maarten belongs to the French and the Dutch. Choices **b** and **d** have no support in the passage. Choice **a** is incorrect. The Spanish are only mentioned in the passage in conjunction with the Indians.

196. d. The idea of the passage is to convince the reader that the metaphor is a wonderful poetic device. None of the other choices are approached in the passage.

197. a. The first paragraph clearly states that poets use metaphors more than any other type of figurative language, thereby inferring that a metaphor is a type of figurative language. Choice **b** is incorrect since the phrase *other type of figurative language* is clearly stated. Choice **c** is not supported in the passage. Choice **d** is incorrect; review the definition of a metaphor in the first and second lines of the passage.

198. c. This detail is presented in the second paragraph. This links thorns with the idea of adding another dimension to the image of love. Choices **a** and **b** are not supported in the passage. Choice **d** is incorrect because thorns are not being compared to a rose.

199. d. The explanation of the line details how love can be wonderful and yet, with the introduction of the thorn imagery, it also presents the danger of love. Choices **b** and **c** are not mentioned in the passage. Choice **a** only deals with the idea of joy, disregarding the thorn/danger aspect.

200. c. This specific detail can be found in paragraph 1. " . . . poets compose their best poetry to express what they are experiencing emotionally at that moment." Choices **a** and **b** are incorrect because they each deal with only one reason for a poet to write. Choice **d** is incorrect since the only discussion of the senses dealt with the specific metaphor that was used as an example.

201. c. This title most nearly captures the main idea of the passage and the author's purpose in writing

the piece. The other choices either are not mentioned or are secondary ideas in the passage.

202. c. The passage clearly states that Wolfgang took an interest in the clavier when his sister was learning to play the instrument.

203. b. In the second paragraph, the passage states that Wolfgang's first *public* appearance was at Linz and that after this concert, word of his genius traveled to Vienna. This paragraph also states that Vienna was the *capital* of the Hapsburg Empire.

204. d. The passage does not say anything about Wolfgang preferring one instrument to another.

205. b. The third paragraph states that at the time, it was not uncommon for child prodigies to have extensive concert tours. The other choices are not supported by the information given in the passage.

206. a. The main point of the passage is to describe Mozart's experiences as a child prodigy, or a highly talented child. Choices **b**, **c**, and **d** are not mentioned in the paragraph.

207. c. The titles in choices **a**, **b**, and **d** all imply that the passage will provide information, which it does not. Choice **c** is the most accurate choice because the passage deals mainly with remembering the fair.

208. a. Sentence 1 (choice **a**) contains the phrase *should have been a colossal failure*, which is an opinion of the author. The other choices are sentences that provide factual information about Woodstock.

209. a. The sentence preceding and leading into sentence 3 speaks of the very brief time—a month—that the organizers of the fair had to find a new site and get information out. Choices **b** and **d** are incorrect because they could not have been known about at the time the fair was moved. Choice **c** is incorrect because there is no indication in the passage that New York officials tried to stop the fair.

▶ SECTION 6 Nonfiction and Information Passages

210. d. The passage details the proper locations for smoke detectors and is ordered according to topic.

211. b. Although the passage mentions firefighters' responsibilities (choice **a**), the main focus of the passage is the installation of smoke detectors. Choice **c** is only a detail. Choice **d** is not mentioned.

212. b. The answer can be found in the first sentence of the third paragraph. Choice **a** may seem attractive because the passage contains the words *four inches* and *twelve inches*, but close reading will show it to be incorrect.

213. a. The answer is found in the first paragraph (*smoke detectors reduce the risk of dying in a fire by half*).

214. c. The answer can be found in the next to last sentence of the passage.

215. d. The answer is implied by the first sentence of the passage. There is no information in the passage to indicate that the other choices are a firefighter's responsibility, even though they may be in certain real-life situations.

216. b. The second paragraph states that there should be a smoke detector *outside each sleeping area* in a home. The last sentence states that smoke detectors should not be placed in kitchens (choice **d**).

217. b. Ideas are listed by topic, but there is some cause and effect as well since the passage explains the reasons for the various steps. The other choices are incorrect because the passage does not list the ideas in order of importance (hierarchical) or in the order in which they have occurred or should occur (chronological). These steps can occur in any order.

218. c. The passage does say that a homeowner can have an energy audit, but it says nothing about a local energy company providing that service. Choice **a** may seem attractive at first since those specific figures are not mentioned in the passage, but the third paragraph does say that fluorescent bulbs can save 50% on lighting costs, and $65 is almost 50% less than $135. Choices **b** and **d** are clearly stated in the passage.

219. a. The passage is offering recommendations about the many things homeowners and renters can do to save money and energy. The other choices may all be mentioned in the passage, but they are too specific to be the main idea.

220. d. The passage says nothing about an energy auditor actually fixing the flaws him- or herself, simply that the auditor will locate the flaws and offer possible money-saving solutions.

221. a. The fifth paragraph states that double-paned windows can cut energy costs, so we can infer that this means that they are energy efficient. The other three choices are not stated in the passage.

222. a. The passage is organized chronologically. The steps for starting a book club are listed in the order in which they should occur.

223. c. The second sentence of the second paragraph states this clearly.

224. d. Deciding on the club's focus—the kinds of books or genre the club will read—should be done prior to this meeting and prior to recruiting members, according to the second paragraph.

225. b. This is the only appropriate title. Choice **a** is too specific, since the passage indicates that making new friends is just one component of a book club. Choice **c** is incorrect because this passage does not contain numbered steps. Choice **d** is too vague, and the tone is inappropriate.

226. a. The passage states this is one possible focus but does not say successful book clubs must focus exclusively on one genre. The other choices are all in the passage. Choice **c** might seem attractive at first, but the passage clearly states that a focus should be chosen, even if that focus is defined as flexible and open.

227. d. The tone and specificity of the passage infer that a successful book club requires careful planning.

228. d. This is a listing of reasons why Hartville employees are unhappy and went on strike.

229. c. The second sentence of the second task-force finding states that Hartville's equipment does not meet current health and safety standards. Choices **a** and **b** may be attractive at first, but choice **a** is incorrect because it doesn't say the equipment is broken, just that it is old and dangerous. Choice **b** is incorrect because computer keyboards are not mentioned, and there is no indication that computer keyboards are included in the equipment being discussed.

230. d. The only specific recommendation in the task-force findings appears in the second finding regarding equipment in the manufacturing department, in the final sentence.

231. b. The final finding of the task force states that due to the withholding of information by middle management, upper management is unaware of the severity of employee discontent. The other choices are not stated in the passage.

232. d. The third task-force finding states that sick and personal day policies are unclear, and no outline of an actual policy is provided.

233. c. Choice **c** provides the best outline of the passage. The other choices all contain points that are not covered by the passage.

234. b. This passage provides information to social workers about music therapy, as the title in choice **b** indicates. Choice **d** is incorrect because the first sentence speaks of mental- and physical-health professionals *referring* their clients and patients to music therapists; the second sentence indicates that *it* (meaning a *referral*) *seems a particularly good choice for the social worker.* Choice **c** is possible, but does not summarize the passage as well as choice **b**. Choice **a** refers to a topic not covered in the passage.

235. d. Although the other choices may be correct, they require knowledge beyond the passage. Based on the information in the passage, **d** is the best choice.

236. a. Based particularly on the last sentence of the passage, **a** is the best choice. The other choices are beyond the scope of the passage.

237. d. In the Northern Hemisphere, June 21 would be summer; however, according to the passage, it is the beginning of winter in the Southern Hemisphere.

238. b. Logically, if June 21 is called the summer solstice in the Northern Hemisphere, then that same day would be the winter solstice in the Southern Hemisphere.

239. d. Because the author mentions that one of the two women gained international fame because she attended the international conference, the reader can surmise that for a woman to attend was a rare occurrence; therefore, choice **d** is the best answer. Choices **b** and **c** are beyond the scope of the passage. Choice **a** might be true but would require information not contained in the passage.

240. d. See the final sentence of the passage.

241. d. Answer **d** is the most accurate conclusion because the first sentence speaks of *periods of war.* The other choices, whether true or false, are not addressed in the selection.

242. d. Although the people in the other choices might read this passage, it is not directed toward scholars (choices **a** and **b**), nor is there anything in it about operating a loom (choice **c**). The light, informative tone, as well as the subject matter of the final sentence, particularly indicate that the passage is directed toward interior decorators.

243. a. Choices **c** and **d** are beyond the scope of this passage and a reader would not be able to tell if the author believed them, based on the information provided. Choice **c** reflects a point of view that would be unlikely for the author based on the content of this passage, which implies that the author believes that women and men have an equal need for education.

244. b. The missing sentence is in a portion of the passage that discusses the long-term impacts of the Franks; therefore, **b** is the best choice. Choices **a** and **c** are written in a style appropriate to the passage, but the information is not appropriate. Choice **d** is more informal in style than the rest of the passage.

245. b. Although all of the choices are possible definitions of *culture,* the passage is speaking of a community of interrelated individuals, namely, Europeans.

246. a. The passage explicitly states that Charlemagne was crowned emperor in 800 and died in 814—a period of 14 years. Therefore, **b, c,** and **d** are mathematically incorrect.

247. b. The phrase *ill effects of* that precedes the words *erosion* and *putrefaction* means that putrefaction is a negative consequence, as is erosion. The other choices are either neutral or positive.

248. d. This passage is written in a style directed to a general audience; therefore, choice **b** is not correct, as an advanced marine biology textbook would contain a more specialized style and level of writing. Choice **a** is incorrect because the subject of the passage is not history. This passage is not a personal essay, so choice **c** is also incorrect.

249. c. The second sentence of the second paragraph states that, while corals are the main components of reef structure, they are not the only living participants.

250. b. The context of the passage indicates that the sentences in question are pointing out an unforeseen consequence (*however*) and the current situation (*now*). The other choices would result in meanings that do not fit with the flow of information in the rest of the passage.

251. d. Choices **a, b,** and **c** are not supported by information in the passage. Thus, the best choice is **d**.

252. d. Choices **a** and **c** are possible definitions of *ushered,* but do not fit in the context of the passage. Choice **b** is an incorrect definition. *Heralded,* choice **d**, is the best definition in the context.

253. b. The blank is followed by a discussion of the shortcomings of the RDA approach. Choice **a** is incorrect because it does not lead into a discussion regarding the RDA approach's shortcomings. Choice **c** is incorrect because it is contradicted by the final sentence of the passage, which states that the RDA approach remains a *useful guide.* Choice **d** is incorrect because its casual style is inconsistent with the style used in the rest of the passage.

254. b. Choice **b** is indicated by the final sentence, which indicates that the RDA approach is useful, but has limitations, implying that a supplemental guide would be a good thing. Choice **a** is contradicted by the final sentence of the passage. Choice **c** is incorrect because the passage says the RDA approach is a *useful guide,* but does not say it is the best guide to good nutrition. Choice **d** is contradicted by the next to last sentence of the passage.

255. b. The passage contains objective information about accounting such as one might find in a textbook. There is nothing new or newsworthy in it (choice **a**). The passage does not contain the significant amount of personal opinion one might find in an essay (choice **c**). It does not deal with matters that might involve government (choice **d**).

256. **d.** The final sentence emphasizes the importance of correct interpretation of financial accounting. Choice **a** is wrong, because something so important would not be discretionary (optional). Choice **b** may be true, but it is not as important for guidelines to be convenient as it is for them to be rigorous. Choice **c** is wrong because the word *austere* connotes sternness. People may be stern, but inanimate entities, such as guidelines, cannot be.

257. **b.** Choices **a, c,** and **d** are all listed in the passage as functions of accounting. On the other hand, the second sentence of the passage speaks of a *marketing department*, separate from the *accounting department*.

258. **a.** The final sentence is an instance of a regular pattern that still has an uncanny quality. Choices **b** and **c** would introduce a sentence with an idea contradicting the preceding. Choice **d** would indicate that the final sentence is a restatement of the preceding, which it is not.

259. **d.** The passage says that people in general consider genius *supernatural, but also . . . eccentric*; the pairing of *extraordinary* and *erratic* in choice **d** includes both meanings given in the passage. Choices **a** and **c** cover only one side of the passage's meaning. Choice **b** contains definitions that the passage does not ascribe to the common view of genius.

260. **c.** This title covers the main point of the passage that, although there are predictable patterns in the lives of geniuses, the pattern increases the sense of something supernatural touching their lives. Choices **a** and **b** are too general. Choice **d** is inaccurate because the passage does not talk about disorder in the life of a genius.

261. **c.** All the other statements are inaccurate.

262. **a.** This choice sticks to the subject, Daniel O'Connell. It provides a transition to the sentence following it by giving information about the location of the statue. Choices **b** and **c** swerve off topic, and choice **d** essentially repeats information given elsewhere in the paragraph.

263. **d.** The title *Sights and History on Dublin's O'Connell Street* touches on all the specific subjects of the passage: the sights to see on this particular street and the history connected to them. Choice **a** is too general about the place described, which is a particular street in Dublin, not the whole city. Choices **b** and **c** are too specific in that they cover only the material in the first paragraph.

264. **c.** The hidden or key resource mentioned in the passage is the fine distinction between the definition of *street* and *boulevard*, which is used to win the argument with or *get the better of* tourists. Choices **a** and **b** do not make sense; answer **d** is incorrect because there is no real fraud used in the argument in the passage.

265. **d.** The author offers an example of Dublin wit and mentions the *unhurried* pace of Dublin crowds. Choice **a** interprets the adjective *unhurried* in too negative a manner for the tone of the passage. Answers **b** and **c** similarly interpret the playful joke on French tourists too disparagingly.

266. **a.** This is implied in the first passage, which says that Dilly's is "popular," and the same idea is explicitly stated in the second passage.

267. **d.** This is the only one of the choices that is implied in both passages.

268. **d.** This is the only quotation from the second passage that reveals the critic's opinion of the quality of the food.

269. **a.** The fact that the overall tone of the passage is quite negative indicates the writer's purpose.

270. c. In contrast to the second passage, the first passage seems to be encouraging a visit to Dilly's. Answers **a, b,** and **d** are not mentioned in the passage.

271. d. Choice **d** sums up the first paragraph, which is essentially a list of the cuttlefish's characteristics. It gives the most interesting characteristic, and the sentence introduces the subject of the second paragraph—the ability of the cuttlefish to change color. Choice **a** adds information not in keeping with the tone or focus of the passage. Choice **b** repeats information in the first paragraph but does not introduce the next one. Choice **c** uses but does not explain scientific language, which is out of keeping with the general informational style of the passage.

272. b. The passage describes the cuttlefish's use of a water jet to move. Choice **a** is incorrect because the passage only describes cuttlefish as *resembling* squid. Choice **c** is a true characteristic but is not mentioned in the passage. Choice **d** is incorrect because the passage never describes cuttlefish as the *most* intelligent cephalopod.

273. d. Choice **d** covers the most important ideas in the two paragraphs. All the other choices choose minor details from the paragraphs as the main subjects.

274. d. Choice **d** includes both the informational content and light tone of the passage. Choices **a** and **b** describe too scientific an aim for the content and tone. Choice **c** does not include the informational content of the passage.

275. d. This answer is broad enough to support all the information discussed in the passage: chemicals in the home, research on certain houseplants, the suggestion of the best plants for the job and why. Choice **a** only deals with contaminants. Choice **b** suggests our allergies are caused by chemicals in the home, when the passage suggests that we unknowingly blame our symptoms on allergies. Choice **c** suggests that the passage is only about plants in the home.

276. c. This is explicitly stated in the passage. Choice **a** is an incorrect assumption, as the passage does not discuss allergies; it states that we dismiss the symptoms, blaming allergies as the cause. Choice **b** is tempting, but it is not a specific effect of the chemicals combining; it merely states that ridding our homes of impurities seems a great task. Choice **d** is incorrect because the combination of harmful chemicals does not trigger the process of photosynthesis in any way.

277. a. It is clearly stated that research has been done using *certain* houseplants. Choice **b** is incorrect because the sentence that deals with NASA suggests that *even* NASA is conducting experiments. Choice **c** reveals a faulty reading of the passage in which three of the chemicals are clearly named. Choice **d** is incorrect because the main idea of the passage is for the benefit of homeowners.

278. b. This answer is inferred in the last line of the passage: *primal qualities . . . ability to purify their environment.* Choices **a** and **c** are incorrect because *antiquity* refers to how long the species has been on the planet, which has no relationship to how long a life span the individual plants or leaves have. Choice **d** is incorrect. One cannot make a general statement on how successful the plants' reactions are in research experiments when the passage only presents us with one type of research experiment.

279. c. This title focuses on the main idea of the passage: purifying one's home of chemical impurities by using common houseplants. Choice **a** is incorrect because only one experiment is discussed, and no mention of the millennium is made at all. Choice **b** is also incorrect because the passage only discusses one problem: impurities caused by chemicals, which is not even labeled as a danger. Choice **d** is supported by two sentences in the passage, but it is not broad enough to support all the information offered in the passage.

280. c. The passage best reflects this choice.

281. a. The passage supports this choice only.

282. d. According to the passage, this is the only correct choice.

283. c. The purpose of Egyptian pyramids was to house the dead forever.

284. c. This choice is the only answer supported in the passage.

285. d. Hughes was influenced by jazz music.

286. d. This choice is stated in the passage.

287. a. All other choices are not stated in the passage.

▶ SECTION 7 Reading Charts and Graphs, Understanding Directions

288. c. A wind speed of 143 miles per hour falls between 113 and 157, which is the range for an *F2 tornado*, choice **c**.

289. b. Applying words such as *mild, moderate, significant, severe, devastating, incredible,* and *inconceivable* to the damage done by a tornado is a means of describing the damage, therefore, the words are *descriptive,* choice **b**.

290. b. The Voorhees fire occurred on June 7. The Cougar Run fire occurred on June 14.

291. b. 115 acres at Burgaw Grove and 320 acres at Hanesboro Crossing adds up to 435 acres.

292. d. This is the only choice that is an act of nature. Choice **a** is arson. Choices **b** and **c** are accidents.

293. c. Parkston, with 74 days, is at level three.

294. a. Chase Crossing is at level four; Kings Hill is at level two.

295. a. The question asks in what field the most men are *involved,* not *employed.* The answer would include students, who are not necessarily salaried workers. Therefore, combining the number of students and teachers gives the largest number involved in education.

296. b. Only two of the 200 men in the Baidya caste are farmers.

297. a. The Men's and Women's table shows this as the only correct response.

298. c. The Men's table shows this as the only correct response.

299. d. The Men's and Women's table shows this as the only correct response.

300. b. This choice is reflected in both the Men's table and the Men's and Women's table.

301. d. This is the only correct choice as stated in the chart.

302. c. According to the chart, this is the correct choice.

303. a. This is the correct response for the yearly average.

304. c. The correct response for this month is 7.9 inches.

305. d. The risk, based solely on BMI, is very high.

306. a. This range shows the only minimal health risk.

307. d. Heart rate does not appear on the chart.

308. c. Moderate is the only choice in the second column for health risk based solely on BMI.

309. a. The second sentence states that routine maintenance is performed by the maintenance department.

310. c. The first sentence states that workers are responsible for refueling at the end of each shift; this implies that vehicles are refueled at the end of every shift.

311. d. The second sentence of the passage indicates that each driver who finishes a route will clean a truck.

312. a. The third sentence of the passage indicates that routes vary in the length of time they take to complete. The other choices are not included in the passage.

313. c. According to the last sentence of the passage, in the past, city workers usually drove the same truck each day.

314. a. See the first sentence of the passage.

315. b. The third sentence tells what drivers should do *if the bus is ahead of schedule.* The passage does not mention choice **a** or **c**, and the passengers' complaints have nothing to do with how the bus "runs."

316. d. The whole passage deals with methods drivers should use to keep their buses from running ahead of schedule.

317. c. According to the passage, hazardous waste is defined by the U.S. Environmental Protection Agency (EPA).

318. d. The directions imply that Harris should call the supervisor.

319. d. See paragraph 1. (Paragraphs 2 and 3 make it clear that the Vehicle Maneuvering Training Buses are simulators.)

320. a. See the second sentence of paragraph 2.

321. b. See the last sentence of the fourth paragraph.

322. c. Virtually, the whole passage deals with F.A.S.T. membership requirements. The other choices are too narrow to be main ideas.

323. a. See the first paragraph.

324. c. The specific focus of this passage is stated in the first sentence. It introduces the topic of the sprained ankle. Choice **a** is only one detail of the passage; the entire passage does not describe sprains. Choice **b** is incorrect because there are only two sentences that deal with bandaging, and they only mention ankle sprains. Choice **d** also focuses on only one detail of the passage.

325. d. This is explicitly stated in the fourth sentence of paragraph 1. Choice **a** is not supported by the passage, because enlarged blood vessels are not discussed. Choice **b** is not the cause of a sprain. This was an explanation of the danger of keeping an ice pack on the wound for too long. Choice **c** confuses two details: The ball of the foot is used as the starting point for wrapping the bandage, tissue is not mentioned, and *torn* describes damage to the ligament.

326. c. Choices **a, b,** and **d** are all clearly stated in the passage as warnings. Only **c** is not supported by the passage. *Ankle* and *fire* appear in the same sentence, but only to describe the pain of the injury.

327. d. The passage explicitly states that once the first cold pack is removed, one should wait 30 minutes and then reapply for another 20 minutes. Choice **a** is incorrect because it is not the next step, but the third. Both choices **a** and **b** bypass the reapplication of the cold pack. Choice **c** has the timing of the packs reversed.

328. c. This is implied in the sentence, *bleeding, hence bruising . . .*, demonstrating a clear relationship between bleeding and the "black-and-blue" of the question. Choice **a** is not a direct cause of the bruising; again, blood is. Choice **b** is incorrect because the passage states that wrapping the bandage too tightly will interfere with circulation to the foot, which is the opposite of the condition needed for bruising. Choice **d** is irrelevant to the passage.

▶ SECTION 8 Analyzing and Interpreting Poems

329. b. The eagle, who *watches from his mountain walls* and falls *like a thunderbolt*, is depicted as too alert and dynamic to be dying (choice **a**). There is really no joy depicted in the poem nor any sense that this is a baby eagle (choice **c**), and there is no mention of baby birds the eagle might be watching over (choice **d**). Saying that the eagle *watches* and then falls *like a thunderbolt* implies alertness and then striking, respectively. The most logical choice is that the eagle is hunting.

330. b. The word *azure* means *blue* and is often used to describe the sky. Neither a forest nor cliffs are azure (choices **a** and **c**), and nature is not mentioned as an entity in the poem (choice **d**).

331. a. It is the *wrinkled sea* that *crawls* in the first line of the second stanza of the poem.

332. b. The *fellow* frightens the speaker—**a, c,** and **d** are not frightening.

333. a. *Tighter breathing* indicates fear, as does *zero at the bone* (one is sometimes said to be cold with fear). Also, the subject is a snake, which is generally a feared animal.

334. c. In context, the speaker is discussing animals, because he follows with his contrasting attitude toward *this fellow*, meaning the snake. The other choices are all human beings.

335. b. Stanza 3 contains the phrase *when a boy* implying the speaker was a boy in the past and is now, therefore, an adult man.

336. b. The poem describes nature in terms of the murder of a happy flower, and includes the words *beheads* and *assassin*; therefore, the most logical description of the poet's attitude would not be *delight, indifference,* or *reverence,* but rather *dismay.*

337. c. The flower in the poem is *happy* and feels *no surprise* that it must die, which implies *acceptance.* If there is any hint of *fear* or *horror* in the poem (choices **a** and **b**), it is on the part of the poet. Nothing in the poem is described as feeling *reverence* (choice **d**).

338. c. A God who would approve of a happy flower being beheaded, while, apparently, the rest of the natural world (as exemplified by the sun) remains unmoved, is probably not to be regarded as benevolent or just (choices **a** and **b**). Approval does not connote anger (choice **d**). The most logical choice is that, in this poem, God is cruel (choice **c**).

339. b. Line 2 of stanza 1 states that Death *kindly stopped* for the speaker. Therefore, Death is presented as a kindly gentleman. Choice **a** is incorrect because *indifferent* would suggest that Death did not acknowledge the speaker. Choice **c** is incorrect because the poem does not relate that the character, Death, is an immortal god. Choice **d** (none of the above) is incorrect because **b** is the correct answer.

340. c. This choice fits the kindness of Death, as stated by the speaker, as well as the fact that Death *knew no haste.* Also it includes the idea that the speaker *put away . . . labour and leisure, too, for his civility.* This supports the image of Death as gentle, timeless, and *leaving of life's cares behind.* Choice **a** is a violent image of Death that is not supported by the poem, that is, the image of a kidnapper. Choice **b** is not an idea presented by the poem, but rather one the reader may hold of Death's journey. Choice **d** is not broad enough to support all the ideas of Death that are presented in the poem; it just refers to the last line.

341. b. The meaning of the word can be derived from the context of the line. Because he is driving slowly, *Death knows no haste.* This is a matter of opposites. None of the other choices are the opposite of *slowly.*

342. c. The *swelling of the ground . . . the roof scarcely visible . . . [the cornice] but a mound.* All of these are descriptive of a grave with its gravestone. Choice **a** presents the idea of blurring the worlds of life and death. This is not supported, even with the line that says the *roof was scarcely visible.* This does not mean it was blurred. Choice **b** is incorrect for the same reason that **a** was. Choice **d** is incorrect because the speaker is already dead when she sees the *mound* as anyone would have to be before he could view his grave.

343. a. Death is a pleasant companion; the speaker only describes it in positive, gentle terms. Choice **b** is incorrect because an intruder, someone to be feared, would come from outside. Neither is the case in this poem. Choices **c** and **d** are not supported in the poem.

344. d. The poet uses *merely* to simply make a statement with no emotion attached to it. Therefore, the other answers are all incorrect as anger, amusement, and sorrow are emotions.

345. a. The soldier's behavior is *aggressive*: cursing, jealous of others who receive honor, quick to fight. The lines do not reveal a sense of honor, but rather the soldier's dishonorable behavior. There is no mention of dedication, nor anything to suggest a fear of cowardice.

346. c. The poem begins by stating the "world is a stage" and that we are "merely players." There is no emotion attached to the exits and entrances of man in the poet's tone, thus there is no need for anguish or sorrow. Choice **a** is eliminated by the descriptions of the lover and the justice; there is no misery attached to them. Choice **b** discusses a metaphor of life as a journey down a river, and choice **d** states that life is a comedy. Neither of these choices can be supported by the passage.

347. b. This is supported by the *Last scene of all* in which Shakespeare suggests that old age is a second childhood that will lead to oblivion without control of the senses, like the infant in the first act. Man has come full circle back to his beginning. No fear of death is mentioned, nor is free will, so choices **a** and **d** are incorrect. Choice **c** is incorrect because man is used as the subject of the entries, but never presented as a gender-specific measure.

348. d. The poet accomplishes all three. It softens the effect of both suggestions that we are only actors on the world's stage, and that the seventh age of man results in oblivion. It ties his theme together by carrying us from the first stage to the last and then back again, and the words convey his tone of indifference, as discussed above.

▶ SECTION 9 Philosophy and Literature

349. a. A *scapegoat* is one who is forced to bear the blame for others or upon which the sins of a community are heaped. Choices **b** and **c** are wrong because nowhere in the passage is it implied that Sula is a hero or leader, or even that

the Bottom has such a personage. Sula may be a *victim* (choice **d**), but a community does not necessarily project evil onto a victim or an outcast the way they do onto a scapegoat, so choice **a** is still the best answer.

350. d. The passage says that people who live in the Bottom are *apt to go awry, to break from their prescribed boundaries*. A person who is eccentric is quirky or odd. Nowhere in the passage is it implied that the people are furtive, suspicious, or unkempt (choices **a, b,** and **c**).

351. d. It is logical that a play would close after such a bad first-night reception, and the sentence in choice **d** also uses a metaphor about stage history, which is extended in the next sentence. Choices **a, b,** and **c** do not fit the sense or syntax of the paragraph, because the *however* in the next sentence contradicts them.

352. d. The first line of the passage describes the *English language premiere* of the play, indicating it had previous performances in a different language.

353. a. Although the other choices are sometimes connotations of the term *avant-garde*, the author's meaning of *innovative* is supported by the final judgment of the passage on the play as revolutionary.

354. d. Although the writer seems amused by the negative criticisms of the play, she does give the opinion that it was revolutionary (a word that literally means "a turning point"). Choice **a** underplays and choice **b** overestimates the importance of the work to the author of the passage. Choice **c** is contradicted by the last sentence of the passage.

355. a. The paragraph describes only the similarity between the hero's journey and the poet's. The other choices are not reflected in the passage.

356. d. The first sentence of the passage describes Campbell's hero as *archetypal*. An archetype is a personage or pattern that occurs in literature and human thought often enough to be considered universal. Also, in the second sentence, the author of the passage mentions the *collective unconscious of all humankind*. The faces in the title belong to the hero, not to villagers, countries, or languages (choices **a, b,** and **c**).

357. a. The passage states that the hero's tale will enlighten his fellows, but that it will also be dangerous. Such a story would surely be radically mind altering. Choice **b** is directly contradicted in the passage. If the hero's tale would terrify people *to no good end*, it could not possibly be enlightening. There is nothing in the passage to imply that the tale is a warning of catastrophe or a dangerous lie (choices **c** and **d**).

358. b. The definition of the word *boon* is *blessing*. What the hero brings back may be a kind of gift, charm, or prize (choices **a, c,** and **d**), but those words do not necessarily connote blessing or enlightenment.

359. c. The word *awe* implies mingled reverence, dread, and wonder, so the adjective *awesome* is the best of all the choices to describe a place that is *dangerous and full of wonders* (second sentence of the second paragraph). Choices **a** and **b** both describe a part of the hero's journey but neither describes the whole of it. Choice **d** is incorrect because the hero's journey is described in very serious terms, not in whimsical (playful or fanciful) terms at all.

360. d. The last sentence in the passage says that *the kingdom of the unconscious mind* goes down into *unsuspected Aladdin caves*. The story of Aladdin is a fairy tale (choice **b**), but neither this nor the other choices are in the passage.

361. d. The tone of the passage is one of anticipation and excitement.

362. b. A stagecoach rider is narrating the story.

363. a. All the statements can be supported in the passage except this choice.

364. c. The passage reflects all of the choices except this one.

► SECTION 10 Longer Passages

365. b. Choice **b** includes the main points of the selection and is not too broad. Choice **a** features minor points from the selection. Choice **c** also features minor points, with the addition of "History of the National Park System," which is not included in the selection. Choice **d** lists points that are not discussed in the selection.

366. d. Choice **d** expresses the main idea of paragraph 4 of the selection. The information in choices **a, b,** and **c** is not expressed in paragraph 4.

367. a. Choice **a** is correct, according to the second sentence in paragraph 2. Choices **b** and **c** are mentioned in the selection, but not as causing the islands. Choice **d** is not mentioned in the selection.

368. c. Paragraph 4 discusses the visitors to Acadia National Park, therefore, choice **c** is correct. Choices **a, b,** and **d** are not mentioned in the selection.

369. a. The first sentence, paragraph 3 states that the length of the Maine coastline is 2,500 miles. Paragraph 1 states that a straight-line distance between the northernmost and southernmost coastal cities—not the length of the coastline—is 225 miles, so **c** is incorrect. Choices **b** and **d** are also incorrect.

370. a. This is the best choice because each paragraph of the passage describes an inventor whose machine was a step toward the modern bicycle. There is no evidence to support choice **b**. Choices **c** and **d** are incorrect because they both make statements that, according to the passage, are untrue.

371. d. The fourth paragraph states that *James Starley* added a gear to the pedals.

372. d. The passage gives the history of the bicycle. Choice **a** is incorrect because few opinions are included in the passage. There is no support for choices **b** and **c**.

373. b. This information is clearly stated in the second paragraph. The iron rims kept the tires from getting worn down, and, therefore, the tires lasted longer. Choice **a** is incorrect because although the iron rims probably did make the machine heavier, that was not Macmillan's goal. Choice **c** is incorrect because no information is given about whether iron-rimmed or wooden tires moved more smoothly. There is no support for choice **d**.

374. b. Based on the paragraph, this is the only possible choice. Starley *revolutionized* the bicycle; that is, he made many innovative changes. Based on the context, the other choices make no sense.

375. a. This is the only choice that states an opinion. The writer cannot be certain that the safety bicycle would look familiar to today's cyclists; it is his or her *opinion* that this is so. The other choices are presented as facts.

376. d. The first two sentences of the passage indicate that a backdraft is dangerous because it is an explosion. The other choices are dangers, but they do not define a backdraft.

377. b. The second paragraph indicates that there is little or no visible flame with a potential backdraft. The other choices are listed at the end of the second paragraph as warning signs of a potential backdraft.

378. c. This is stated in the last paragraph. Choice **a** is not mentioned in the passage. The other choices would be useless or harmful.

379. a. The passage indicates that hot, smoldering fires have little or no visible flame and insufficient oxygen. It can reasonably be inferred, then, that more oxygen would produce more visible flames.

380. d. This is stated in the last paragraph (. . . *first aid measures should be directed at quickly cooling the body*). The other responses are first aid for heat exhaustion victims.

381. b. This is stated in the first sentence of the second paragraph. Choices **a** and **c** are symptoms of heat stroke. Choice **d** is not mentioned.

382. a. Heat stroke victims have a *blocked sweating mechanism*, as stated in the third paragraph.

383. b. This information is given in the second paragraph: If the victim still suffers from the symptoms listed in the first sentence of the paragraph, the victim needs more water and salt to help with the *inadequate intake of water and the loss of fluids* that caused those symptoms.

384. d. Many asthma sufferers have an inherited tendency to have allergies, referred to as *atopy* in the third paragraph.

385. b. The fourth sentence of the second paragraph explains that during an attack the person afflicted with asthma will compensate for constricted airways by breathing a greater volume of air.

386. c. The first sentence of the passage begins, *No longer*, indicating that in the past asthma was considered an anomalous inflammation of the bronchi. Now asthma is considered a chronic condition of the lungs.

387. b. An exacerbation is usually defined as an *aggravation of symptoms* or *increase in the severity* of a disease. However, in this passage, *exacerbations* is interchangeable with *asthma attacks*.

388. a. Although cramping may occur during asthma attacks, it is not mentioned in the passage. See the bottom half of the second paragraph for a full explanation of the morphological effects of an attack.

389. d. The third paragraph discusses triggers in detail. Although using a fan in the summer months sounds good, an air conditioner is recommended when the pollen count is high. Family pets and cigarette smoke are all distinctly inflammatory to asthma sufferers. Only physical activity is touted as a possible symptom reducer.

390. a. Because asthma symptoms vary throughout the day, relying on the presence of an attack or even just on the presence of a respiratory ailment to diagnose asthma is flawed logic.

391. b. All the individuals listed would glean a certain amount of knowledge from the passage; however, a healthcare professional would find the broad overview of the effects of asthma, combined with the trigger avoidance and diagnosis information, most relevant. A research scientist would likely have all this information already. A mother with an asthmatic child would probably not be interested in the diagnosis protocol. The antismoking activist probably would not find enough fodder in this article.

392. d. According to the last part of the third paragraph, second-hand smoke can increase the risk of allergic sensitization in children.

393. b. See the third paragraph: "One in ten" (10% of) cases of anorexia end in death.

394. a. See the second and third paragraphs for reference to heart problems with anorexia, the fourth and fifth paragraphs for discussion of heart problems with bulimia, and the last paragraph, where heart disease is mentioned, as a risk in obese people who suffer from binge-eating disorder.

395. c. Near the end of the last paragraph, the passage indicates that binge-eating disorder patients experience high blood pressure.

396. d. It is the other way around: 50% of people with anorexia develop bulimia, as stated near the end of the fifth paragraph.

397. b. The first sentence of the fifth paragraph tells us that bulimia sufferers are often able to keep their problem a secret, partly because they maintain a normal or above-normal weight.

398. c. In the second paragraph, the thyroid gland function is mentioned as slowing down—one effort on the part of the body to protect itself.

399. a. According to the second paragraph, dehydration contributes to constipation.

400. b. As stated in the opening sentence of the fourth paragraph, bulimia patients may exercise obsessively.

401. d. See the second sentence of the sixth paragraph. If as many as one-third of the binge-eating disorder population are men, it stands to reason that up to two-thirds are younger women, given that we have learned that about 90% of all eating disorder sufferers are adolescent and young adult women.

402. c. The tone of the passage is enthusiastic in its recommendation of the greyhound as pet and, thereby, encourages people to adopt one. It does not give advice on transforming a greyhound (choice **a**). Except to say that they love to run, the passage does not spend equal time on describing the greyhound as racer (choice **b**). The author's tone is not objective (choice **d**), but rather enthusiastic.

403. d. See the last paragraph. The passage does not mention **b** or **c**. Choice **a** is clearly wrong; the passage states the opposite.

404. a. See the first paragraph. Choices **b, c,** and **d** are not touched on in the passage.

405. d. See the last paragraph. Choices **a, b,** and **c** are contradicted in the passage.

406. d. The enthusiastic tone of the passage seems meant to encourage people to adopt retired greyhounds. Choice **a** is wrong because there is only one statistic in the passage (in the first sentence), and it is not used to prove the point that greyhounds make good pets. Choice **b** is wrong because the author substantiates every point with information. Choice **c** is wrong because the passage does make the negative point that greyhounds do not make good watchdogs.

407. b. See the end of the next to last sentence in the passage. Choices **a, c,** and **d** are not to be found in the passage.

408. b. This is stated explicitly in the second sentence of the passage. Choice **a** is incorrect because only bad eris was defined as violent. Choice **c** deals with problems that belong in the domain of mankind, not the universe. Choice **d** has no support in the passage.

409. a. Again, this is a definition explicitly stated in the sixth sentence. Choice **b** is incorrect because a choice dealing with mankind alone is too narrow for a definition of eris, which deals with the entire universe. Choice **c** is incorrect because it only deals with one action of the personified concept in goddess form. Choice **d** has no support.

410. d. This is stated in the third sentence of paragraph 2. Zeus did not want to sire [father] a child who could eventually overthrow him. According to the passage, he felt it was safer to arrange for the child's father to be a mortal. There is no support in the passage for any of the other choices.

411. c. This answer follows the logic of the previous answer. A mortal *child could never challenge the gods* implies that Zeus feared that if the child were immortal, it would overthrow him. The other choices mention individual words that appear in the passage but have no support.

412. b. The second to the last line in paragraph 2 tells us that Achilles was the son of Thetis and Peleus, and that the war will result in his death. Choice **a** is incorrect because there is no other mention of Zeus or events in the Trojan War other than Achilles' death. Choice **c** is incorrect because Eris purposely created the conditions that would lead to the war to kill the child of the bride and groom. Choice **d** is incorrect because Achilles is the son of Thetis and Peleus, the bride and groom of the myth.

413. c. This lesson is discussed explicitly in paragraph 3. All other choices are irrelevant.

414. c. The husband had a civil servant's job and received a steady salary; the wife had a servant who cleaned for her. The couple lived in a dwelling that had several rooms. This implies that they lived comfortably. Choice **a** is incor-

rect because they obviously were not impoverished. Choice **b** is incorrect because the wife had a maid. Choice **d** is incorrect because this was the life the wife wanted to have, but instead had *shabby walls, worn furniture* etc.

415. d. This question relates to the previous one. This choice presents the fact that the wife had a maid. Choice **a** does not deal with the couple's economic standing, but only the wife's before she was married. Choice **b** is tempting, but the poverty of her rooms is more in her eyes than a truthful economic indicator. How poverty stricken can she be if she has a maid? Choice **c** deals with a tablecloth that has been used three days in a row. It has nothing to do with economic standing because it could have been washed by the maid or the wife, and the situation would have been remedied.

416. a. It is obvious from the description of the wife's thoughts in the first paragraph that she wished she had married a rich man. Instead, she *slipped into marriage with a minor civil servant.* The woman is ashamed of her marriage and of her husband's occupation to the point of making it sound like an accident, as one may slip on a wet floor. Choices **b, c,** and **d** are incorrect because the wife loving anything other than expensive things is never mentioned in the passage.

417. b. The husband's delight with the homemade stew only seems to send his wife into another bout of daydreams to escape her middle-class prison. Choice **a** is blatantly incorrect, because the husband obviously enjoys homemade beef stew while the wife dreams of wings of grouse. Choice **c** is incorrect because the husband is either unaware of his wife's anguish or doesn't let it affect his delight in his dinner. Choice **d** is irrelevant to the passage.

418. d. This is reinforced by the last two sentences of the passage. The wife admits she only loves rich things, believes she was made for them, and focuses all her desires on being *admired and sought after*, thinking only of herself at all times. Choice **a** is incorrect because the author paints a negative picture of the wife. Although choice **b** is tempting, the author does not develop the husband enough for him to become the focus of the passage. Choice **c** is incorrect because it is not developed in the passage. The focus is on the wife, not on class distinctions in general.

419. a. Adjectives are the words that describe nouns. These are the words that truly add dimension to the descriptions of the home and the daydreams of the wife. *Innate, instinctive, grandest, gorgeous, gleaming,* and *pink* are some of the adjectives that enrich the nouns of the wife's dreams. *Shabby, worn, ugly,* and *homemade* are adjectives that add to the undesirable view she has of her present situation. None of the other choices add such richness to the passage.

420. b. This answer is explicitly stated in the first sentence of the selection. Choices **a** and **d** are not mentioned as a result of plaque-laden arteries. Choice **c** is too general to be the best answer.

421. c. This answer is explicitly stated in the sixth sentence of paragraph 1. Choice **a** only names one medical instrument used during the procedure. Choice **b** offers the reason for the angioplasty, because it is done to compress the plaque in an artery. Choice **d** offers a procedure that would be chosen as an alternative to angioplasty.

422. a. The first and second sentences of paragraph 2 state how both procedures, angioplasty and bypass surgery, are invasive because "both involve entering the body cavity." None of the other choices are supported or implied as a definition for invasive.

423. c. The procedure is detailed in paragraph 3. It begins with injecting a special dye. Choices **a** and **b** follow later in the procedure, whereas choice **d** deals with bypass surgery rather than the angioplasty procedure.

424. d. This answer can be found in paragraph 4. A team of surgeons stands ready to perform bypass surgery even though the risk factor of death is only 2%. Choice **a** is not supported in the passage. Choices **c** and **d** are incorrect because the passage does not discuss patient reaction at all.

425. a. This choice is supported in the last sentence of paragraph 3. Choice **b** is incorrect: The risk factor is 2%. Choice **c** is a complete misunderstanding of the text. Inflating a balloon into a blocked artery is coronary balloon angioplasty. Because two answers are incorrect, **d** is not a viable choice.

426. d. Choices **b** and **c**, meaning scattered and erratic respectively, are not supported in the passage. Choice **a** may be considered a synonym, but it is not the best choice. The best choice is **d**, *requisite*.

427. b. Paragraph 2 of the passage clearly states that Benjamin Franklin first considered the concept of DST.

428. b. Paragraph 3 states that the bill (which was introduced by Sir Robert Pearce in 1909) met with great opposition, mostly from farmers.

429. d. This choice is directly supported by paragraph 5.

430. a. Choices **b** and **c** are incorrect because they each refer to specific points raised in the passage, but not throughout the passage. Choice **d** is too broad to represent the best title. Only choice **a** describes the point of the entire passage.

431. c. Paragraph 5 clearly states that during the oil embargo and energy crisis of the 1970s, President Richard Nixon extended DST through the Daylight Saving Time Energy Act of 1973 to conserve energy further.

432. b. This is an inference question. The writer indicates that visitors to Hershey's Chocolate World are greeted by a giant Reeses Peanut Butter Cup, so it is logical to assume that these are manufactured by Hershey. Although the writer mentions the popularity of chocolate internationally, you cannot assume that it is popular in every country (choice **a**), nor is there any indication that Milton Hershey was the first person to manufacture chocolate in the United States (choice **c**). Choice **d** is not discussed in the passage at all.

433. d. This question tests your ability to use context clues to determine the intended meaning of a word. In paragraph 3, the passage says, *The Hershey Chocolate company was born in 1894 as a subsidiary of the Lancaster Caramel Company*. This indicates that a subsidiary is one controlled by another company, choice **d**. Although it may be true that Milton Hershey owned each company in its entirety (choice **a**), that is not clear from the material. There is also no indication that the chocolate company was created to support the caramel company (choice **b**). Finally, the passage contains no discussion of whether or not any of Hershey's companies were incorporated (choice **c**).

434. a. Choice **a** is the best choice because it is the most complete statement of the material. Choices **c** and **d** focus on small details of the passage; choice **b** is not discussed in the passage.

435. b. Paragraph 3 states that Hershey sold the caramel company six years after the founding of the chocolate company. The chocolate company was founded in 1894; the correct choice is **b**.

436. c. The Chicago International Exposition was where Hershey saw a demonstration of German chocolate-making techniques, which indicates, along with the word *international* in its title, that the exposition contained displays from a variety of countries, choice **c**. None of the other choices can be inferred from the information in the passage.

437. b. There is nothing inherently dramatic, undignified, or rewarding discussed in paragraph 1. *Modest* is the word that best fits being born in a small village and having the unremarkable

early life described; it is also a word that provides a contrast to the mention of Milton's later popularity.

438. d. The second sentence of paragraph 1 states that probes record responses. Paragraph 2 says that electrodes *accumulate much data*.

439. c. The tone throughout the passage suggests the potential for microprobes. They can be permanently implanted, they have advantages over electrodes, they are promising candidates for neural prostheses, they will have great accuracy, and they are flexible.

440. d. According to the third paragraph, people who *lack* biochemicals could receive doses via prostheses. However, there is no suggestion that removing biochemicals would be viable.

441. a. The first sentence of the third paragraph says that microprobes have channels that *open the way for delivery of drugs*. Studying the brain (choice **d**) is not the initial function of channels, though it is one of the uses of the probes themselves.

442. b. Throughout, the passage compares and contrasts the various methods of medical waste disposal.

443. d. See the last sentence of paragraph 3. Compaction may well reduce transportation costs (choice **a**) according to paragraph 3. That it reduces the volume of waste (choice **b**) is an advantage, not a disadvantage. Compaction is not designed to eliminate organic matter, so confirming that it has been eliminated (choice **c**) is not an issue.

444. a. See the last sentence of paragraph 5, which states that *incineration is . . . the preferred method for on-site treatment*.

445. b. See the last sentence of paragraph 6, which points out that steam sterilization does not change the appearance of the waste, thus perhaps raising questions at a landfill.

446. c. Paragraph 4 states that liquid is separated from pulp in the hydropulping process. Paragraph 6 says that liquid may form during the sterilization process.

447. a. This response relies on an understanding of pathological wastes, which are wastes generated by infectious materials. Paragraph 7 points out that incineration is especially appropriate for pathological wastes. Previously, paragraph 6 had said that steam sterilization is appropriate for substances contaminated with infectious organisms.

448. d. The second paragraph says that the main risk of pushing carts is potential exposure from torn bags but that automated carts can reduce that potential.

449. b. See the next to last sentence of paragraph 4. Sterilization does not change the appearance of waste. Although compacting does change the volume of the waste, it is not appropriate for eliminating hazardous materials.

450. d. See the second sentence of paragraph 2: *. . . there is some risk of exhausting contaminants into hallways*, meaning waste might be discharged.

451. b. See the last sentence of the passage, which states that *the costs have been prohibitive for smaller units* when using rotary kilns.

452. c. Although the contaminants may sometimes be extremely toxic (choice **a**), the word *fugitive* here is the key to the meaning. The words *fugitive emissions* are used in the context of the disposal process of hydropulping. To be a fugitive means to run away or to escape, so the logical choice, given this context, is choice **c**. There is nothing anywhere in the passage about criminal activity, so choice **b** is not a likely answer. Choice **d** is wrong because the microbiological testing of which the passage speaks pertains to ensuring that all waste is disposed of.

453. c. According to the paragraph 2, *Deep, underlying fissures* that *already existed in the economy* led to the Great Depression.

454. a. The passage is primarily an account that describes the causative factors (for example, tariff and war-debt policies, disproportionate wealth, and the accumulation of debt) that led to the Depression and its effects (for example, business failures, bank closings, homelessness, federal relief programs).

455. c. Paragraph 1 states that shantytowns were called *Hoovervilles* because citizens blamed their plight on the Hoover administration's refusal to offer assistance.

456. b. Although policies can refer to regulations or *laws* (choice **c**) or guiding principles or *theories* (choice **a**), in this context, *policies* refers to the courses of action that are taken, from which a government or business intends to influence decisions or actions. Choice **b** is the only answer that implies action.

457. d. The passage describes the decade as one in which spending dominated over prudent measures like saving (paragraph 3). The wild stock market speculation, also described in that paragraph, is another example of extravagance.

458. b. The analogy depicts the stock market crash of 1929 as a weakening agent to the economy (the way a stressful event may weaken the body's resistance to illness).

459. d. This paragraph clearly states that the New Deal expanded the role of the central government in regulating the economy and creating social assistance programs. Choices **b** and **c** are incorrect and choice **a** requires an opinion; the author does not offer his or her viewpoint about the New Deal measures.

460. a. Choice **b** emphasizes only damage to the atmosphere; the passage encompasses more than that. Choice **c** does not mention the atmosphere, which is the main focus of the passage. Choice **d** is too narrow—the final paragraph of the passage emphasizes that the circulation of the atmosphere is but one example of the complex events that keeps the earth alive.

461. c. This question assesses the ability to see the organization of a reading passage and to organize material for study purposes. Choice **a** is wrong because the passage does not explain exactly what will happen as a result of damage to the atmosphere and other life-sustaining mechanisms. Choice **b** is wrong because the passage does not explain the origin of the atmosphere. Choice **d** is wrong because it is solar energy that travels 93 million miles through space, not the atmosphere.

462. b. The *biosphere*, as defined in paragraph 1, is a *region* (or part) of the earth; it is not the envelope around the earth, the living things on Earth, or the circulation of the atmosphere (choices **a, c,** and **d**).

463. d. This question assesses the ability to recognize supported and unsupported claims. Choice **a** deals with solar radiation, not with circulation of the atmosphere. Choice **b** is an assertion without specific supporting detail. Choice **c** describes how the atmosphere protects Earth but does not speak of the circulation of the atmosphere. Only choice **d** explains that conditions would be inhospitable at the equator and poles without the circulation of the atmosphere; therefore, it is the best choice.

464. a. This question assesses the ability to see cause and effect. Paragraph 2 deals with how variations in the strength with which solar radiation strikes the earth affects temperature. None of the other choices is discussed in terms of all temperature changes on Earth.

465. a. There is no mention in the first paragraph of any *reviving* or *cleansing* effect the atmosphere may have (choices **b** and **d**). In a sense, enabling the earth to sustain life is invigorating; however, choice **a** is a better choice because the first two sentences talk about how the atmosphere *protects* the earth from harmful forces.

466. b. Paragraph 1 mentions that the symptoms of Type II diabetes may occur gradually and thus be attributed to other causes. Left untreated, diabetes can cause damage to several major organs in the body.

467. b. According to the beginning of paragraph 2, only the long-term health problems are the same for these two different disorders.

468. d. Paragraph 2 mentions that when the body has more glucose than needed, it stores the overflow in muscle tissue, fat, or the liver.

469. c. According to the last paragraph, non-insulin-dependent diabetics should stick to a diet consisting of 50–60% carbohydrates. The paragraph also notes that raw foods do not cause as high a blood sugar level as cooked foods.

470. a. Paragraph 4 mentions that, although insulin must bind to a receptor in order to begin working, the main role of insulin is to signal the burning of glucose/sugar for energy. Most hormones function as stimuli for other processes.

471. b. Type II, or non-insulin-dependent, diabetes is the main subject of the passage, which distinguishes Type II from Type I and goes on to stress the importance of diet.

472. d. Paragraph 4 of the passage tells us that possible problems with insulin receptors include a paucity of receptors or a defect causing improper binding of the insulin to the receptors. In addition, even though insulin may bind to its receptors, cells may fail to read the signal to metabolize the glucose.

473. c. Paragraph 2 states that normally, after the digestive system breaks down food into smaller molecules, including glucose (otherwise known as sugar), the blood-sugar level rises. Insulin is then released from the pancreas, thus signaling tissues to metabolize the glucose.

474. c. Type I diabetes is the insulin-dependent form of this condition. The minority of diabetics are afflicted with this form. They are diagnosed as children and must take daily injections of insulin to compensate for what their pancreases do not produce.

475. a. The final paragraph says that there is no cure for diabetes, so choices **b** and **d** are incorrect. Choice **c** is a possibility, but consider the sound of the word *soothe*. It does not fit with the objective tone of the passage nearly as well as the word *counteract*.

476. c. In the first paragraph, the communication network of the millions of cells in the immune system is compared to bees swarming around a hive.

477. b. All the answers indicate peaceful coexistence. However, according to the fifth sentence of paragraph 2, in this instance, the state is referred to as *self-tolerance*.

478. c. See the last paragraph. The substances known as *allergens* are responsible for triggering an inappropriate immune response to ragweed pollen.

479. d. The last paragraph of the passage mentions that an antigen announces its foreignness with intricate shapes called *epitopes* that protrude from the surface.

480. a. Every individual's immune system must learn to recognize and deal with non-self molecules through experience. However, the last section of paragraph 2 mentions that the immune system is capable of choices **b, c,** and **d.**

481. b. According to paragraph 2, the ability to distinguish between self and non-self is the heart of the immune system. This topic is set up in the first paragraph and further elucidated throughout the body of the passage.

482. b. The last paragraph mentions that tissues or cells from another individual may act as antigens except in the case of identical twins whose cells carry identical self-markers.

483. a. The context leads to the meaning: The first sentence speaks of complexity, from which we can infer an elaborate system of interconnections,

especially in light of the second sentence. There is no mention of confusion in the passage (choice **b**). The word *perplexity* means bewilderment and is unrelated to the passage (choice **c**). Choice **d** is a newspaper and TV term that is unrelated to the passage.

484. b. The crow is using the stick as a tool to assist it in getting food.

485. a. In the first paragraph, *upsurge* (a swelling of the ocean) is used as an analogy to illustrate the large and increasing amount of research in animal intelligence.

486. c. The questions in this paragraph ask the reader to consider the use of animals in our world and questions whether knowing that they have more intelligence than previously thought might make a difference in human treatment of them.

487. d. This choice is the only one that shows animals using human language.

488 c. Although each conclusion is an example of some intelligence, the most accurate conclusion the reader should make is that this action shows high intelligence. The complexity of what the chimpanzee is doing to get his food and the many thinking activities he must accomplish in order to realize his goal of getting the termites—learning a new skill, selecting and shaping a tool, remembering stored knowledge, using the correct knowledge in order to take proper action for the situation—shows intelligence.

489. b. Cuing does not demonstrate animal intelligence because the animal learns to do or not to do certain things by following outside signals.

490. d. One of the hazards of living in a city near a glacier is the possibility that lakes forming on top of the glacier may flood the city. Although the other answers are all true statements, none describe negative effects.

491. a. This passage states that although most glaciers are in remote regions, some are nearby. The reader needs to understand that the transitional word *however* indicates that the word *remote* means the opposite of *near*.

492. c. The passage states that glaciers can be found on nearly every continent.

493. b. This is the only choice reflected in the passage.

494. b. This choice is the only one that can be concluded from the passage.

495. a. Many examples in the last paragraph suggest the large potential of untapped electrical power that may be harnessed from glacial water in the future with further research.

496. b. Although all choices are true statements, only **b** states the main idea.

497. d. Statements **a, b,** and **c** appear in the passage; this statement does not.

498. b. The passage only gives evidence that supports this answer.

499. d. This is the best definition that describes Anthony's efforts.

500. c. Although each statement is true, her greatest and lasting achievement was that her efforts led to the establishment of the nineteenth amendment.

501. b. This is the only choice that the passage supports.

NOTES